Dillard's Presents

Southern Living®
YEAR-ROUND
Celebrations
cooking · entertaining · giving

Oxmoor House®

CONTENTS

TABLE SETTINGS

YEAR-ROUND MENUS

CELEBRATE YOUR FAVORITE YEAR-ROUND
HOLIDAYS

Usher in a year of festive entertaining inspired by the parties and decorating ideas on the following pages. Four seasons of delicious menus take the guesswork out of hosting and ensure a perfectly polished, memorable gathering from start to finish.

NATURAL BEAUTY

Pair a fresh green-and-white palette and organic textures with a few elegant details for an outdoor table with all the opulence of its indoor counterpart.

❶ White table linens and fine china, typically reserved for indoor use only, up the style factor outside. Keep formality in check by mixing in warm accents like wood-handled flatware and rattan-covered tumblers. ❷ Create a verdant centerpiece by grouping dampened florist foam blocks on a round platter, trimming edges to fit. Secure blocks with florist tape. Loop English ivy vines from the yard around the foam, and tuck stems of white hydrangeas and 'Polo' roses into the top. ❸ Personalized paperweights are ideal outdoor place cards that won't blow away, and they make great party favors, too. Make your own at photoweights.com. ❹ Save yourself trips to the kitchen by staging items you might need during the meal (such as extra water, wine, linens, and condiments) on a console table nearby.

Highlights

A chandelier hung from a tree branch over the table is an elegant accent. Wire into existing outdoor lighting or, for an unwired alternative, try a candlelit lantern.

Details

Think beyond the table linens. A graphic monogram boldly embellishes the back of this Louis XVI dining chair.

SPRING FOR A GARDEN PARTY

*Welcome the season by setting a vibrant table
in a range of fresh hues and fine linens.*

1 Hand-painted scarab place cards paired with potted wheatgrass reinforce the garden theme. **2** Jewel tones make a bold impression. A sapphire topper with an aquamarine appliqué border is a striking backdrop for all the other colors at play. **3** Even when you're thinking outside the box, mix in classics. Old standbys, such as silver flatware, ground a contemporary scheme. **4** Pastel macarons, almost too pretty to eat, match the table's hues. Layering napkins between the plates looks elegant and makes serving easy.

PUNCH UP YOUR PORCH

*There's nothing like outdoor entertaining on your front porch—
it's the epitome of spring in the South.*

1 A pretty floral, stately monogram, and bold pops of green are a fresh backdrop for blue-and-white Willow china.
2 Drawer pulls act as holders for the bamboo-bordered place cards. (Tighten the washers to keep the cards secure.)
3 Granny Smith apples, lemon leaf, and hydrangeas combine in a seamless mix of country elegance and chinoiserie chic. **4** A dessert station stocked with iced sugar cookies and a three-tier cake tempts guests as they arrive.

Eclectic

Use odds and ends. Shawls or leftover fabrics make great table runners. Why use plastic cutlery when mismatched silverware from estate sales costs the same (or less)?

CELEBRATE FALL

Paper plates are fine for a picnic. But when it comes to gracious entertaining outdoors, step it up a notch. Transport the elegance of an indoor affair to a picturesque spot on a porch, next to a live oak, or out in the open beneath the stars. The good news is that elevating outdoor entertaining to an art form isn't about spending (or stressing) more; it's about incorporating thoughtful details.

1 Suspend a rustic "candelier" over the table to create a flickering glow and ambience. **2** Glass offertory candles burn forever and double as hurricanes on windy nights. Wrap them in vintage ledger pages with rosemary and twine. **3** Create a stocked "walk-up bar" through an open window with a server inside making drinks to order.

PILE ON THE PUMPKINS

Look to nature's pretty autumn palette. Decorate with fall leaves, glowing pumpkins, and cool-season vegetables and greens from the garden.

1 The 10-minute votives: Feel free to skip the container and place the votives anywhere that could use a little fall glow. How to do it: Fill a rustic container two-thirds full of water. Use a craft knife to trace circles a little larger than the bottom of a tea light onto orange mini pumpkins. Cut and carve out the circles to allow a candle to fit inside comfortably. Insert tea lights. Float pumpkin votives as well as whole pumpkins in water. Using the photo as a guide, add bright fall leaves and sprigs of herbs for color and texture. **2** Simple and rustic, this quick-to-make arrangement delivers an easy "wow." How to do it: Wrap twine several times around votive holders and colorful fall leaves, and secure with a knot. To construct different heights, top the votive holders with varying numbers of small white pumpkins. Add a touch more autumn dazzle to your display with this simple addition: Gather an assortment of colorful fall leaves, and use wire to fasten them to a length of rope to form a beautiful seasonal garland. Using temporary adhesive hooks, attach the leaf garland to your mantel.

Drama

Wow them with color. Stagger vases the length of the table and fill with an explosion of bright blooms. Remove the tallest vases before guests are seated so they can easily converse across the table.

EXTRAORDINARY ARRANGEMENTS

Impressing discriminating house guests is no easy feat. Find inspiration with these stylized approaches to holiday botanical focal points.

1 A pineapple ice bucket is an alternative vessel for a mélange of tulips, amaryllis, hypericum berries, and Japanese cryptomeria in Palm Beach hues. **2** Twirling topiaries, made from dried hydrangeas, green plums, and scabiosa pods, twist upward toward gilded pineapple toppers. **3** Delight Derby-lovers with rose-filled trophies accented with green and red berries, ranunculus, and sprigs of pine. **4** This pretty sideboard tableau bridges autumn and winter with freesia, bells-of-Ireland, and verdant tea tree paired with feathers, antlers, and bone-handled cutlery.

Blackberry Pisco Sours, page F34

Shrimp Boil with Green Olives and Lemon, page F45

Spicy Pumpkin Soup with Avocado Cream, page F71

Strawberry Shortcake, page F60

YEAR-ROUND MENUS

Fancy or casual, large or small, we've got inspiration for four seasons of occasions to keep the party going all year long.

EASTER POTLUCK

*Shared contributions make this special holiday a memorable feast.
Enlist your guests to bring a favorite recipe to fit your menu needs. Swap
recipes at the end of the gathering to have a great keepsake from the day.*

Menu

Rose's Asparagus, Spring Onion, and Feta Quiche

Wade's Potato Salad

Julia's Spring Pasta Bake

Pam's Citrus Cupcakes

Dad's Chocolate Truffle Pie

ROSE'S ASPARAGUS, SPRING ONION, AND FETA QUICHE

SERVES 6 · HANDS-ON: 30 minutes · TOTAL: 2 hours, 30 minutes

Vegetable cooking spray
1 (14.1-ounce) package refrigerated piecrusts
2 tablespoons salted butter
2 cups thinly sliced spring onions
1 bunch fresh asparagus, trimmed and cut into 1-inch pieces

2 teaspoons kosher salt
¾ teaspoon ground black pepper
1 cup heavy cream
8 large eggs
2 tablespoons thinly sliced chives

2 tablespoons chopped flat-leaf parsley
⅛ teaspoon ground nutmeg
¾ cup crumbled feta cheese

1. Preheat the oven to 425°F. Lightly grease a 10-inch deep-dish tart pan with removable bottom with cooking spray. Unroll piecrusts; stack on a lightly floured surface. Roll stacked piecrusts into a 12-inch circle. Fit piecrust into prepared tart pan; press into fluted edges. Trim off excess piecrust along edges. Line piecrust with aluminum foil or parchment paper, and fill to rim with pie weights or dried beans. Place pan on a baking sheet. Bake at 425°F for 14 minutes. Remove weights and foil, and bake at 425°F for 10 to 12 minutes or until golden brown. Reduce oven temperature to 350°F. Cool the piecrust completely on a baking sheet on a wire rack (about 15 minutes).

2. Meanwhile, melt the butter in a skillet over medium-high. Add the onions, and cook, stirring occasionally, about 10 minutes or until tender and lightly browned. Stir in the asparagus; sprinkle with ½ teaspoon of the salt and ¼ teaspoon of the pepper. Remove from heat, and cool 5 minutes.

3. Whisk together the cream, eggs, chives, parsley, nutmeg, and remaining salt and pepper.

4. Place half the onion mixture (about 1 cup) in tart shell; sprinkle with ¼ cup of the feta. Spoon half of the cream mixture (about 1½ cups) over feta. Repeat; sprinkle top with remaining ¼ cup feta.

5. Bake at 425°F for 1 hour or until set. Cool on a baking sheet on a wire rack 20 minutes before serving.

WADE'S POTATO SALAD

This colorful salad includes a produce basket of springtime's tender harvests.

SERVES 8 · HANDS-ON: 20 minutes · TOTAL: 1 hour, 15 minutes

SALAD:
- 2 (12-ounce) packages fresh green beans
- ¾ teaspoon table salt
- 1 pound petite red potatoes
- 1 large yellow bell pepper, cut into thin strips
- ⅓ cup thinly sliced red onion

LEMON-SOY VINAIGRETTE:
- ¼ cup firmly packed light brown sugar
- ¼ cup fresh lemon juice
- 2 tablespoons soy sauce
- 2 teaspoons sesame oil
- ½ teaspoon dried crushed red pepper
- 3 tablespoons chopped fresh mint
- 2 tablespoons toasted sliced almonds
- 1 tablespoon toasted sesame seeds

1. Make the salad: Cook the green beans and ½ teaspoon of the salt in boiling water to cover in a large saucepan until crisp-tender, 3 to 4 minutes; drain. Plunge into ice water to stop the cooking process; drain and pat dry with paper towels.

2. Bring the potatoes and cold water to cover to a boil in large saucepan over medium-high; reduce heat to medium-low, and simmer about 20 minutes or until just tender. Drain and cool 30 minutes. Slice potatoes into ¼- to ½-inch rounds.

3. Gently toss together green beans, potatoes, bell pepper, red onion, and remaining ¼ teaspoon salt in a large bowl.

4. Make the vinaigrette: Whisk together the brown sugar and next 4 ingredients. Add the vinaigrette to bean mixture, and gently toss to combine. Transfer the mixture to a serving platter, and top with mint, almonds, and sesame seeds. Serve at room temperature or chilled.

How to Plan a Potluck

CHOOSE A THEME: Let guests know if you're planning a formal holiday buffet or a casual Tex-Mex fiesta. No one wants to set a disposable aluminum pan of baked beans next to a trifle served in Grandma's finest china.

KNOW YOUR NUMBERS: Decide how many appetizers, sides, and desserts you will need based on the number of people attending. If you have 20 guests and two are making desserts, they should each prepare something that serves at least 10 people. However, before dessert, most guests won't eat a full portion of a dish when other options are on the table.

ASK GUESTS TO SIGN UP: To avoid ending up with too much of one thing, make a list—two green vegetables, three starches, one chocolate dessert—and ask guests to choose one. Communicate this however you feel comfortable: Make phone calls, e-mail a sign-up sheet, or use an online service. (We recommend signupgenius.com/potluck.)

MAKE SPECIAL REQUESTS: If your crowd will be looking forward to Aunt Susan's famous squash casserole, then ask her to bring it to the party.

LABEL DISHES: Personalize your table by letting guests know what they're digging into and who made it.

PREP YOUR SERVEWARE: There's a good chance someone will forget to bring a serving utensil for their dish, so be prepared with the essentials like salad tongs, pie servers, and slotted spoons.

PLAN FOR LEFTOVERS: Should guests divide up any food that remains? Are to-go plates approved? Leave it up to the person who made the dish. Stock up on extra paper plates, aluminum foil, and plastic wrap so you're also prepared for the meal's end.

JULIA'S SPRING PASTA BAKE

SERVES 8 · **HANDS-ON:** 25 minutes · **TOTAL:** 1 hour, 5 minutes

PASTA:
Vegetable cooking spray
4 ounces (½ cup) salted butter
½ cup (2.25 ounces) all-purpose flour
2 teaspoons dry mustard
1 teaspoon table salt
½ teaspoon ground black pepper
¼ teaspoon ground red pepper
2 cups half-and-half
2 cups whole milk

1 (16-ounce) block Swiss cheese, shredded
2 ounces Parmesan cheese, shredded (about ⅔ cup)
1 (16-ounce) package farfalle (bow-tie pasta), prepared according to package directions

1 (12-ounce) package cubed boneless ham (about 2 cups)
1½ cups frozen baby sweet peas, thawed

TOPPING:
1 cup sea salt-and-pepper croutons
2 ounces Parmesan cheese, shredded (about ⅔ cup)
1 tablespoon butter, melted

1. Make the pasta: Preheat the oven to 350°F. Grease a 12- x 9-inch baking dish with cooking spray. Melt the butter in a Dutch oven over medium. Gradually add in the flour until smooth; cook, whisking constantly, 2 minutes. Add the dry mustard, salt, black pepper, and red pepper. Gradually whisk in the half-and-half and milk; cook, whisking constantly, 8 to 10 minutes or until thickened.

2. Whisk in the Swiss cheese and 2 ounces Parmesan cheese. Remove from heat. Stir in the pasta, ham, and peas. Pour the mixture into prepared baking dish.

3. Make the topping: Process croutons and 2 ounces Parmesan cheese in a food processor until finely ground. Add 1 tablespoon melted butter; process until combined. Sprinkle over pasta mixture.

4. Bake at 350°F for 30 minutes or until golden. Let stand 10 minutes.

PAM'S CITRUS CUPCAKES

Tart and sweet, these cupcakes delight young and old alike; plus, there are enough for seconds.

MAKES about 30 cupcakes · HANDS-ON: 30 minutes · TOTAL: 1 hour, 10 minutes

CUPCAKES:
- 30 paper baking cups
- 8 ounces (1 cup) butter, softened
- 2½ cups granulated sugar
- 6 large eggs
- 3 cups (13.5 ounces) all-purpose flour
- 1 teaspoon baking powder
- ½ teaspoon baking soda
- ¼ teaspoon table salt
- 1 (8-ounce) container sour cream
- 1 tablespoon lemon zest
- 1 tablespoon fresh lemon juice
- 1 teaspoon vanilla extract

FROSTING:
- 8 ounces (1 cup) butter, softened
- 3 tablespoons lemon zest
- 1 (32-ounce) package powdered sugar
- 8 to 9 tablespoons fresh lemon juice
- 1 to 2 drops of yellow liquid food coloring

1. Make the cupcakes: Preheat the oven to 350°F. Place 30 paper baking cups in 3 (12-cup) standard-size muffin pans.

2. Beat 1 cup softened butter at medium speed with a heavy-duty electric stand mixer until creamy; gradually add granulated sugar, beating until light and fluffy. Add the eggs, 1 at a time, beating just until blended after each addition.

3. Stir together the flour, baking powder, baking soda, and salt. Add the flour mixture to butter mixture alternately with sour cream, beginning and ending with flour mixture. Beat at low speed just until blended after each addition. Stir in 1 tablespoon zest, 1 tablespoon juice, and 1 teaspoon vanilla. Spoon ¼ cup batter into each prepared baking cup.

4. Bake at 350°F for 20 to 23 minutes or until a wooden pick inserted in centers comes out clean. Remove from pans to wire racks, and cool completely (about 20 minutes).

5. Make the frosting: Beat the butter and lemon zest at medium speed with a heavy-duty electric stand mixer 1 to 2 minutes or until creamy. Gradually add the powdered sugar alternately with 8 tablespoons of the lemon juice, beating at low speed until blended after each addition. Add up to 1 tablespoon lemon juice, 1 teaspoon at a time, beating until desired consistency is reached. Add food coloring, and beat at high speed 1 to 2 minutes until well blended and frosting is light and fluffy.

6. Spoon the frosting into a zip-top plastic freezer bag. Snip 1 corner of bag to make a small hole. Pipe about 1½ tablespoons frosting onto each cupcake.

LIME SHERBET CUPCAKES

Substitute lime zest for lemon zest and fresh lime juice for lemon juice. For frosting, substitute fresh lime juice for lemon juice, and 1 to 2 drops of green liquid food coloring for yellow.

ORANGE SHERBET CUPCAKES

Substitute orange zest for lemon zest and fresh orange juice for lemon juice. For frosting, substitute orange zest for lemon zest and 1 tablespoon lemon juice and 7 to 8 tablespoons fresh orange juice in place of 8 to 9 tablespoons lemon juice. Substitute 1 drop of orange liquid food coloring for yellow.

DAD'S CHOCOLATE TRUFFLE PIE

Decadently rich, a thin wedge is enough to satisfy and pairs well with an espresso.

SERVES 8 · HANDS-ON: 25 minutes · TOTAL: 3 hours

CHOCOLATE TRUFFLE PIE:
- ½ (14.1-ounce) package refrigerated piecrusts
- 1 cup (6 ounces) semisweet chocolate morsels
- 1 cup (6 ounces) bittersweet chocolate morsels
- 4 ounces (½ cup) butter, softened

- ¾ cup firmly packed light brown sugar
- 3 large eggs
- 1 teaspoon vanilla extract
- ¼ teaspoon almond extract
- ½ cup (2.25 ounces) all-purpose flour
- 1 cup toasted slivered almonds

AMARETTO CREAM:
- 1 cup heavy cream
- 2 teaspoons almond-flavored liqueur
- ¼ cup powdered sugar

1. Make the pie: Preheat the oven to 350°F. Fit the piecrust into a 9-inch pie pan; fold edges under, and crimp. Line the piecrust with aluminum foil or parchment paper, and fill to rim with pie weights or dried beans. Place pan on a baking sheet. Bake at 350°F for 10 minutes. Remove weights and foil, and bake at 350°F for 10 to 12 more minutes or until bottom is lightly browned. Cool on baking sheet on a wire rack while preparing filling.

2. Microwave the semisweet and bittersweet chocolate morsels in a small microwave-safe bowl at MEDIUM (50% power) 3 to 4 minutes or until melted and smooth, stirring at 30-second intervals. Cool 15 minutes.

3. Beat the butter and brown sugar at medium speed with an electric mixer until light and fluffy. Add the eggs, 1 at a time, beating after each addition. Stir in the melted chocolate and the extracts; stir in the flour and toasted almonds. Spread the mixture evenly in pastry shell.

4. Bake at 350°F for 30 to 35 minutes or until set, covering edges with aluminum foil during the last 10 minutes to prevent overbrowning, if needed. Cool completely on a wire rack (about 1 hour). Chill 1 hour.

5. Make the cream: Beat the cream and liqueur at medium-high speed with an electric mixer until foamy. Gradually add the powdered sugar, beating until soft peaks form. Chill 1 hour. Serve pie with the Amaretto Cream. Store leftover pie, covered, in refrigerator.

DERBY PARTY

Don your fancy hat and raise an icy julep glass to high stakes fun.

Menu

Cucumber Mint Julep

Chilled Sweet Pea Soup with Mint and Cream

Jalapeño Cheese Straws

Pork Tenderloin Sliders

Bourbon-Spiked Honey Custard with Berries

CUCUMBER MINT JULEP

Slice a cucumber lengthwise with a vegetable peeler into thin ribbons for muddling in the bottom of the julep glass. Add fresh mint, mint simple syrup, and your favorite Kentucky bourbon and it's time for a toast.

SERVES 1 · HANDS-ON: 10 minutes · TOTAL: 10 minutes, plus 24 hours to chill syrup

MINT SIMPLE SYRUP:
1 cup sugar
1 cup water
10 to 12 fresh mint sprigs

MINT JULEP:
1 cucumber ribbon
3 fresh mint leaves
1 tablespoon Mint Simple Syrup
Crushed ice
1½ to 2 tablespoons (1 ounce) bourbon

1 (4-inch) cocktail straw or coffee stirrer
1 fresh mint sprig
Powdered sugar (optional)

1. Make the syrup: Bring the sugar and 1 cup water to a boil in a medium saucepan. Boil, stirring often, 5 minutes or until sugar dissolves. Remove from heat; add 10 to 12 fresh mint sprigs, and cool completely. Pour into a glass jar; cover and chill 24 hours. Remove and discard mint.
2. Make the mint julep: Place the cucumber ribbon, 3 mint leaves, and 1 tablespoon Mint Simple Syrup in a chilled julep cup. Muddle the cucumber, mint, and syrup in the cup to release flavors. Pack cup tightly with crushed ice; pour bourbon over ice. Insert straw, place the mint sprig directly next to straw, and serve immediately. Sprinkle with the powdered sugar, if desired.

NOTE: We tested with Woodford Reserve Distiller's Select Bourbon.

CHILLED SWEET PEA SOUP WITH MINT AND CREAM

This bright, minty, make-ahead soup adds a pop of spring color to the buffet.

MAKES 6 cups • **HANDS-ON:** 30 minutes • **TOTAL:** 1 hour

3 medium leeks (white and light green parts only), chopped

1 ounce (2 tablespoons) butter

1 (32-ounce) container reduced-sodium fat-free chicken broth

1 (16-ounce) package frozen sweet peas

¼ cup chopped fresh mint leaves

2 teaspoons kosher salt

½ teaspoon freshly ground black pepper

1 cup sour cream

2 tablespoons fresh lemon juice

Garnish: sliced chives

1. Remove and discard root ends and dark green tops of leeks. Cut in half lengthwise, and rinse thoroughly under cold running water to remove grit and sand.

2. Melt the butter in a large saucepan over medium-low. Add the leeks, and cook, stirring occasionally, 6 to 8 minutes or until tender. Stir in the chicken broth, and increase heat to high. Bring to a boil. Add the peas, and cook, stirring occasionally, 3 minutes or until peas are tender. Remove from heat, and stir in the mint, 2 teaspoons salt, and ½ teaspoon pepper.

3. Process the pea mixture in a blender or food processor until smooth. Transfer to a bowl; whisk in ½ cup of the sour cream. Pour into 2-ounce glasses. Chill 30 minutes to 1 hour. Whisk together the lemon juice and remaining ½ cup sour cream. Dollop on each serving.

JALAPEÑO CHEESE STRAWS

This subtly spicy recipe wowed our Test Kitchen staff!

MAKES about 4 dozen • **HANDS-ON:** 30 minutes • **TOTAL:** 1 hour, 15 minutes

Parchment paper

1 (8-ounce) block extra-sharp Cheddar cheese, grated

¼ cup grated Parmesan cheese

5⅓ tablespoons (⅓ cup) butter, softened

3 tablespoons diced pimiento, drained

1 jalapeño pepper, seeded and minced

2 teaspoons half-and-half

1 teaspoon kosher salt

⅛ to ¼ teaspoon ground red pepper (optional)

1½ cups (6.75 ounces) all-purpose flour

1. Preheat the oven to 350°F. Line 2 baking sheets with parchment paper. Beat the Cheddar cheese, next 6 ingredients, and, if desired, red pepper at medium speed with a heavy-duty electric stand mixer until blended. Gradually add the flour, beating at low speed just until combined.

2. Turn the dough out onto a floured surface. Divide dough in half; flatten halves into squares. Roll to ⅛-inch thickness (about 12 x 12 inches). Cut into 12- x ½-inch strips, using a fluted pastry wheel.

3. Holding 1 dough strip at each end, twist the strip until tightly curled. Pinch ends to seal. Repeat with remaining strips, and place ½ inch apart on prepared baking sheets.

4. Bake at 350°F for 10 minutes, placing 1 sheet on middle oven rack and 1 sheet on lower rack. Rotate pans front to back and top to bottom. Bake 10 more minutes or until edges brown. Cool on baking sheets on wire racks 5 minutes. Remove to wire racks; cool completely.

PORK TENDERLOIN SLIDERS

Slice the tenderloins on a cutting board and set out rolls and condiments for self-service ease.

MAKES 20 sliders · **HANDS-ON:** 25 minutes · **TOTAL:** 55 minutes

ITALIAN-STYLE SALSA VERDE:
- 1 small jalapeño pepper
- 2 medium banana peppers
- ½ cup extra virgin olive oil
- ⅓ cup finely chopped fresh flat-leaf parsley
- 4½ teaspoons chopped fresh chives
- 1 tablespoon minced fresh oregano
- 2 garlic cloves, minced
- 1 teaspoon kosher salt

PORK TENDERLOIN SLIDERS:
- 2 pork tenderloins (about 2½ pounds), trimmed
- 3 tablespoons olive oil
- 2 teaspoons kosher salt
- 1 teaspoon freshly ground black pepper
- ¼ cup packed brown sugar
- 2 tablespoons Dijon mustard
- 3 tablespoons fresh thyme leaves
- 2 tablespoons chopped fresh rosemary
- 20 slider buns or rolls, split

1. Make the salsa: Preheat the broiler with oven rack 6 inches from heat. Broil the jalapeño 3 to 4 minutes on each side or until blackened. Place the blackened jalapeño in a small bowl, cover with plastic wrap, and let stand 10 minutes. Meanwhile, broil the banana peppers 1 to 2 minutes on each side or just until blistered and slightly softened. Cool completely (about 10 minutes), and chop. Peel and finely chop the peppers, discarding seeds.

2. Stir together oil, next 5 ingredients, and chopped peppers in a bowl. Cover; let stand 30 minutes.

3. Make the sliders: Reduce the oven to 400°F. Rub the tenderloins with 1 tablespoon of the oil; sprinkle with the salt and pepper. Stir together sugar and next 3 ingredients; rub over the pork.

4. Cook the pork in remaining 2 tablespoons hot oil in a skillet over medium-high 5 minutes, browning on all sides. Place the tenderloins on a wire rack in a jelly-roll pan.

5. Bake at 400°F for 20 minutes or until a meat thermometer inserted in thickest portion registers 155°F. Remove from oven, and let stand 10 minutes. Slice and serve on the slider buns with the salsa, or wrap tenderloin whole and refrigerate up to 3 days.

BOURBON-SPIKED HONEY CUSTARD WITH BERRIES

If you don't have white balsamic vinegar, substitute Champagne vinegar or apple cider vinegar.

SERVES 8 to 10 • **HANDS-ON:** 30 minutes • **TOTAL:** 30 minutes

1   cup heavy cream
4   large egg yolks
¼   cup honey
⅓   cup Kentucky bourbon

6 to 8 cups mixed fresh berries (such as strawberries, blueberries, blackberries, and raspberries)

Garnish: fresh mint

1. Beat the cream in a medium bowl at medium-high speed with an electric mixer until soft peaks form. Cover and chill until ready to use.

2. Whisk together the egg yolks, honey, and bourbon in the top of a double boiler. Bring water in bottom pan to a light boil. Cook the egg yolk mixture, whisking constantly, 8 to 10 minutes or until thick and foamy.

3. Remove from the heat. Fill a large bowl with ice. Place the top of the double boiler containing the egg yolk mixture in ice, and whisk 5 minutes or until completely cool. Remove from ice bath, and fold in the whipped cream. If desired, cover and chill up to 24 hours. Spoon the berries into bowls, and serve with custard.

A Rose Revival

NO. 1: Select a medium-size footed bowl. It should hold about 4 cups of water.

NO. 2: Fill the bottom with florist foam that has been soaked in water 30 minutes. Cut the foam to fill your container, and make it level with the top edge.

NO. 3: Arrange large roses (garden roses are the most dramatic; we used 13) with 3-inch stems in three even rows, leaving space between each row.

NO. 4: Fill in between the rows with small green spray roses, green chrysanthemums, or lacy reindeer moss.

MOTHER'S DAY LUNCH

Honor the woman of the hour in memorable, al fresco style,
while pulling out all the stops—fine china, crisp linens, and flower-filled vases.

Menu

Spring Pea Pasta with Ricotta and Herbs

Blackberry Pisco Sours

Deviled Potatoes

Kale-and-Collards Salad

Praline Bread Pudding

SPRING PEA PASTA
WITH RICOTTA AND HERBS

*This one-pot primavera brings together seasonal favorites: fresh herbs,
crunchy sugar snap peas, and sweet peas. Combining ricotta cheese with the salty
water left over from boiling the pasta makes a super-easy creamy sauce.*

SERVES 4 · HANDS-ON: 30 minutes · TOTAL: 30 minutes

4   quarts water
¼   cup kosher salt
8   ounces gemelli, penne, or other short pasta
2   (8-ounce) packages sugar snap peas, trimmed and strings removed

1   (13-ounce) package frozen sweet peas, thawed
1   cup ricotta cheese
½   cup firmly packed fresh flat-leaf parsley leaves
1   ounce (2 tablespoons) butter

2   tablespoons thinly sliced fresh chives
2   tablespoons chopped fresh tarragon

1. Bring the 4 quarts water to a boil in a stockpot over high. Add ¼ cup salt; return to a boil. Add the pasta; boil, stirring occasionally, until al dente, about 8 minutes. Stir in the sugar snap peas, and cook 2 minutes. Stir in the sweet peas, and cook 1 minute. Drain the pasta mixture, reserving ½ cup cooking water.

2. Return the pasta mixture to pot. Add the ricotta, parsley, butter, chives, tarragon, and reserved cooking water; stir to coat. Serve immediately.

BLACKBERRY PISCO SOURS

Pisco is a South American grape brandy popular in Peru and Chile. If you can't find it in your area, substitute white tequila, grappa, or vodka. Don't be alarmed by the strength of this new classic; it's a cocktail that's meant to be sipped and savored.

SERVES 4 · HANDS-ON: 15 minutes · TOTAL: 15 minutes

SIMPLE SYRUP:
1 cup water
1 cup sugar

SOURS:
1 cup fresh blackberries
1 cup pisco, chilled
⅓ cup fresh lime juice

3 large pasteurized egg whites
Angostura bitters (optional)
Garnishes: fresh basil leaves, fresh blackberries

1. Make the syrup: Bring 1 cup water and sugar to a boil in a small saucepan over medium, stirring occasionally. Boil 1 minute or until sugar dissolves. Remove from heat, and cool 30 minutes.
2. Make the sours: Process the blackberries in a blender until smooth. Pour through a wire-mesh strainer into a 1-quart jar with a tight-fitting lid, discarding solids.
3. Add the pisco, lime juice, egg whites, and 5 tablespoons of the syrup to jar. Cover with lid, and shake vigorously 30 seconds or until foamy. Pour the mixture into 4 (10-ounce) glasses filled with ice. Top each with a dash of bitters, if desired. Serve immediately.

NOTE: Refrigerate Simple Syrup in an airtight container up to 2 weeks. Use leftover syrup to sweeten iced tea.

DEVILED POTATOES

Two Southern classics, deviled eggs and potato salad, join forces to create these two-bite wonders. Make them a day before your get-together, and chill until you head out. When you arrive, they'll be the right serving temperature.

SERVES 10 · HANDS-ON: 25 minutes · TOTAL: 2 hours

1 pound petite red potatoes (about 15)
1 tablespoon olive oil
1½ teaspoons kosher salt
½ cup sour cream

2 tablespoons brined capers, drained and rinsed
2 teaspoons chopped fresh flat-leaf parsley
2 teaspoons chopped fresh dill

2 teaspoons whole-grain mustard
1 teaspoon lemon zest
Garnish: chopped fresh flat-leaf parsley

1. Preheat the oven to 350°F. Place the potatoes in a small bowl, and drizzle with oil. Sprinkle with 1 teaspoon of the salt; toss to coat. Spread the potatoes in a single layer on a baking sheet, and bake until tender when pierced, about 40 minutes. Remove from oven, and cool 15 minutes.
2. Cut each potato in half crosswise. Carefully scoop out potato pulp into a medium bowl, leaving shells intact. Place the shells, cut side up, on baking sheet, and bake at 350°F for 10 more minutes or until dry. Cool completely (about 30 minutes).
3. Stir together the potato pulp, sour cream, capers, parsley, dill, mustard, zest, and remaining ½ teaspoon salt. Spoon the mixture generously into each potato shell.

**Blackberry
Pisco Sours**

KALE-AND-COLLARDS SALAD

When making this bracing salad, dress the kale and collards in advance to tenderize them.

SERVES 8 to 10 · HANDS-ON: 30 minutes · TOTAL: 1 hour, 35 minutes

1 bunch fresh collard greens (about 8 ounces)
1 bunch Tuscan kale (about 8 ounces)
¾ cup sweetened dried cranberries
3 Bartlett pears, sliced
2 avocados, peeled and diced

1 tablespoon fresh lemon juice
1 small head radicchio, shredded
¾ cup chopped toasted pecans
6 cooked bacon slices, crumbled

LEMON DRESSING:
¼ cup fresh lemon juice
2 garlic cloves, minced
2 teaspoons Dijon mustard
1 teaspoon kosher salt
½ teaspoon freshly ground black pepper
½ cup olive oil

1. Make the lemon dressing: Whisk together the lemon juice and next 4 ingredients in a small bowl. Add the olive oil in a slow, steady stream, whisking constantly until smooth.

2. Make the salad: Trim and discard tough stalks from centers of collard and kale leaves; stack leaves, and roll up, starting at 1 long side. Cut into ¼-inch-thick slices. Toss collards and kale with cranberries and Lemon Dressing in a large bowl. Cover and chill 1 hour.

3. Toss together pears and next 2 ingredients just before serving. Toss pear mixture, radicchio, pecans, and bacon with collard mixture. Serve immediately.

PRALINE BREAD PUDDING

Enjoy this rich and buttery (and decidedly Southern!) ending to any meal.

SERVES 12 · HANDS-ON: 30 minutes · TOTAL: 3 hours

PRALINE BREAD PUDDING:
- 6 large eggs
- 3 cups heavy cream
- 3 cups milk
- 2 cups firmly packed dark brown sugar
- 2 tablespoons vanilla extract
- ¼ teaspoon table salt
- ¼ teaspoon ground nutmeg

- 1 (16-ounce) day-old French bread loaf, cut into 1-inch cubes (about 14 cups)
- 2 cups coarsely chopped toasted pecans
- Vegetable cooking spray

PRALINE SAUCE:
- 3 tablespoons butter

- 1 tablespoon all-purpose flour
- 1 cup heavy cream
- ½ cup firmly packed dark brown sugar
- 2 tablespoons vanilla extract
- ¼ teaspoon ground nutmeg
- ⅛ teaspoon table salt
- Garnish: whipped cream

1. Make the pudding: Whisk together the first 7 ingredients in a large bowl. Add the bread cubes, stirring to coat. Let stand 1 hour, stirring occasionally to ensure an even coating. Stir in the pecans.

2. Preheat the oven to 350°F. Lightly grease a 13- x 9-inch baking dish with cooking spray; pour bread mixture into prepared dish. Bake at 350°F for 1 hour or until bubbly around edges and firm in center, shielding with aluminum foil after 45 minutes to prevent excessive browning.

3. Meanwhile, make the sauce: Melt the butter in a small saucepan over medium-low; whisk in flour, and cook, whisking constantly, 3 to 4 minutes or until foamy and golden brown. Whisk in the cream and brown sugar; cook, whisking constantly, until thickened, about 3 minutes. Whisk in the vanilla, nutmeg, and salt; cook, whisking constantly, until bubbly, 2 to 3 minutes.

4. Let breading pudding stand 5 minutes. Serve with the Praline Sauce.

GRADUATION LUNCHEON

Commemorate a rite of passage celebrated in perfectly Southern style.

Menu

Our Best Southern Fried Chicken

Roasted Shallot Dip

Pickled Shrimp with Fennel

Cracklin' Cornbread

Key Lime Pound Cake

OUR BEST SOUTHERN FRIED CHICKEN

Look no further for that perfect fried chicken recipe. Southerners will find this favorite to be a mouthwatering treasure that they will return to again and again.

SERVES 4 · **HANDS-ON:** 55 minutes · **TOTAL:** 8 hours, 55 minutes

3 quarts water
1 tablespoon table salt
1 (2- to 2½-pound) whole chicken, cut up
1 teaspoon table salt

1 teaspoon freshly ground black pepper
1 cup (4.5 ounces) all-purpose flour

2 cups vegetable oil
¼ cup bacon drippings

1. Combine the 3 quarts water and 1 tablespoon salt in a large bowl; add the chicken. Cover and chill 8 hours. Drain the chicken; rinse with cold water, and pat dry.

2. Combine 1 teaspoon salt and pepper; sprinkle half of the pepper mixture evenly over chicken. Combine remaining pepper mixture and flour in a large zip-top plastic freezer bag. Place 2 pieces of chicken in the bag; seal. Shake to evenly coat. Remove the chicken, and repeat procedure with remaining chicken, 2 pieces at a time.

3. Combine the vegetable oil and bacon drippings in a 12-inch cast-iron skillet or chicken fryer; heat to 360°F. Add the chicken, a few pieces at a time, skin side down. Cover and cook 6 minutes; uncover and cook 9 minutes.

4. Turn the chicken pieces; cover and cook for 6 minutes. Uncover and cook 5 to 9 minutes, turning pieces during the last 3 minutes for even browning, if necessary. Drain on paper towels.

NOTE: For best results, keep the oil temperature between 300° to 325°F as you fry the chicken. Also, you may substitute 2 cups buttermilk for the saltwater solution used to soak the chicken pieces. Proceed as directed.

ROASTED SHALLOT DIP

Caramelized sweet shallots and silky mascarpone cheese add new-school touches to onion-soup dip.
No need to waste time peeling all the shallots; after roasting, the papery skins easily slip away.

MAKES about 4 cups · **HANDS-ON:** 20 minutes · **TOTAL:** 5 hours, 35 minutes

1½ pounds shallots, unpeeled and root ends trimmed
3 garlic cloves, unpeeled
2 tablespoons vegetable oil
Salt and pepper
1 (8-ounce) container sour cream

1 (8-ounce) container mascarpone cheese
⅓ cup thinly sliced fresh chives
1 tablespoon fresh lemon juice
2 teaspoons whole-grain Dijon mustard
¾ teaspoon kosher salt

½ teaspoon freshly ground black pepper
Dash of hot sauce
Garnishes: cooked and crumbled bacon, lemon zest, chopped fresh chives

1. Preheat oven to 425°F. Cut shallots in half. Toss together shallots and next 2 ingredients in a jelly-roll pan; sprinkle with desired amount of salt and pepper. Bake at 425°F for 45 to 50 minutes or until shallots are light brown and skins are charred, stirring twice. Cool completely in pan on a wire rack (about 30 minutes). Remove and discard papery skins from shallots and garlic, and coarsely chop.
2. Stir together sour cream and next 7 ingredients; fold in shallot mixture. Add salt and pepper to taste. Cover and chill 4 to 48 hours. Stir before serving. Add salt and pepper to taste just before serving, if desired.

PICKLED SHRIMP WITH FENNEL

*Marinated plump shrimp and crunchy sliced fennel make great
hors d'oeuvres with wooden picks and an even better no-fuss cold salad.*

SERVES 8 · **HANDS-ON:** 40 minutes · **TOTAL:** 2 hours

1 small fennel bulb
1 tablespoon kosher salt
2 quarts water
2 pounds large raw shrimp,
    peeled and deveined

1 cup fresh lemon juice
½ cup white wine vinegar
1 small serrano or bird pepper,
    seeded and thinly sliced
1½ teaspoons kosher salt

1 teaspoon sugar
1 cup thinly sliced white onion

1. Rinse fennel thoroughly. Trim and discard root end of fennel bulb. Trim stalks from bulb. Slice fennel bulb thinly, reserving fronds. Chop fronds to equal 1 tablespoon. Fill a large bowl halfway with ice and water.

2. Bring 1 tablespoon kosher salt and 2 quarts water to a boil in a Dutch oven over high. Remove from heat; add the shrimp, and let stand, stirring once, 1 minute or just until shrimp turn pink.

3. Transfer the shrimp to ice water, using a slotted spoon. Reserve 2 cups of the hot cooking liquid in a medium bowl. Let the shrimp stand 10 minutes, stirring once. Transfer the shrimp to a paper towel-lined plate, reserving ice water in bowl.

4. Whisk the lemon juice and next 4 ingredients into reserved hot cooking liquid until salt and sugar dissolve. Place bowl in reserved ice water, and whisk lemon juice mixture until cooled to room temperature (about 10 minutes).

5. Remove the bowl of lemon juice mixture from ice water; discard ice water, reserving chilled bowl for shrimp. Stir together the onion, fennel slices, chopped fennel fronds, and shrimp in the chilled bowl. Pour the cooled lemon juice mixture over shrimp mixture. Cover and chill 1 hour to 2 days. Serve with a slotted spoon.

CRACKLIN' CORNBREAD

A true classic, our traditional Southern cornbread calls for just six ingredients.

SERVES 8 to 10 · **HANDS-ON:** 10 minutes · **TOTAL:** 39 minutes

2 ounces (¼ cup) butter
2 cups self-rising cornmeal mix

½ cup all-purpose flour
2½ cups buttermilk

2 large eggs, lightly beaten
1 cup cracklings*

1. Preheat the oven to 425°F. Place the butter in a 9-inch cast-iron skillet, and heat in the oven at 425°F for 4 minutes.

2. Combine the cornmeal mix and flour in a large bowl; make a well in center of mixture. Stir together the buttermilk, eggs, and cracklings; add to dry ingredients, stirring just until moistened. Pour over the melted butter in hot skillet. Bake at 425°F for 25 to 30 minutes or until golden brown.

*1 cup cooked, crumbled bacon (12 to 15 slices) may be substituted for cracklings.

KEY LIME POUND CAKE

*Dress up traditional pound cake with a little lime zest
and a homemade glaze for a deliciously tropical treat.*

SERVES 12 · **HANDS-ON:** 45 minutes · **TOTAL:** 2 hours, 45 minutes

KEY LIME POUND CAKE:
Shortening
8 ounces (1 cup) butter, softened
½ cup shortening
3 cups sugar
6 large eggs
3 cups (13.5 ounces) all-purpose flour
½ teaspoon baking powder
⅛ teaspoon table salt
1 cup milk
1 teaspoon vanilla extract
1 teaspoon lime zest
¼ cup fresh Key lime juice

KEY LIME GLAZE:
1 cup powdered sugar
2 tablespoons fresh Key lime juice
½ teaspoon vanilla extract
Garnish: lime slices, whipped cream, mint sprigs

1. Make the cake: Preheat the oven to 325°F. Grease (with shortening) and flour a 10-inch (12-cup) tube pan. Beat the butter and ½ cup shortening at medium speed with a heavy-duty electric stand mixer until creamy. Gradually add the sugar, beating at medium speed until light and fluffy. Add the eggs, 1 at a time, beating just until blended after each addition.

2. Stir together the flour, baking powder, and salt. Add the flour mixture to the butter mixture alternately with milk, beginning and ending with flour mixture. Beat at low speed just until blended after each addition. Stir in the vanilla, lime zest, and lime juice. Pour batter into prepared tube pan.

3. Bake at 325°F for 1 hour and 15 minutes to 1 hour and 20 minutes or until a long wooden pick inserted in center comes out clean. Cool in pan on a wire rack 10 to 15 minutes; remove from pan to wire rack.

4. Make the glaze: Whisk together the powdered sugar, lime juice, and vanilla until smooth, and immediately brush over top and sides of cake. Cool completely (about 1 hour).

SUMMER SHRIMP BOIL

Welcome the warm weather with a backyard boil that's as low-key as it is Lowcountry.

Menu

Shrimp Boil with Green Olives and Lemon

Roasted Potato-and-Okra Salad

Crispy Andouille Hush Puppies

Boozy Shortcakes with Sweet Cream

ShooFly Punch

SHRIMP BOIL WITH GREEN OLIVES AND LEMON

The simmering liquid is packed with flavor, which transfers nicely to the shrimp.

SERVES 6 to 8 • HANDS-ON: 15 minutes • TOTAL: 55 minutes, including sauces

SHRIMP BOIL:
- 2 medium-size yellow onions, chopped
- 3 celery ribs, chopped
- 4 garlic cloves
- 4 bay leaves
- 8 black peppercorns
- 2 dried chile peppers
- 3 lemons, sliced
- 6 fresh flat-leaf parsley sprigs
- 6 fresh thyme sprigs
- ¼ cup kosher salt
- 4 quarts water
- 3 pounds unpeeled, medium-size raw shrimp
- 1½ cups pitted Spanish olives

SHRIMP SPICE MIX:
- 1½ tablespoons paprika
- 2 teaspoons kosher salt
- 1 teaspoon lemon pepper
- ½ teaspoon dried oregano
- ¼ teaspoon ground red pepper

CLASSIC COCKTAIL SAUCE:
- 1 cup ketchup
- ½ cup prepared horseradish
- 1 tablespoon fresh lemon juice
- 1 tablespoon Worcestershire sauce
- 1 teaspoon hot sauce
- Kosher salt
- Freshly ground black pepper

WHITE COCKTAIL SAUCE:
- ½ cup mayonnaise
- ½ cup sour cream
- ½ cup prepared horseradish
- 1 tablespoon fresh lime juice
- 1 teaspoon thinly sliced chives
- 1 teaspoon Worcestershire sauce
- ½ teaspoon hot sauce
- Kosher salt
- Freshly ground black pepper
- Lemon wedges
- Garnish: fresh flat-leaf parsley sprigs, fresh thyme sprigs

1. Make the shrimp boil: Bring the first 10 ingredients and 4 quarts water to a boil in a large Dutch oven over medium-high. Reduce heat to medium-low; cover and simmer 20 minutes.

2. Add the shrimp to Dutch oven. Increase heat to high, and return to a simmer. Add the Spanish olives. Remove from heat, and cover with a tight-fitting lid. Let stand 5 minutes.

3. Make the spice mix: Stir together the paprika, salt, lemon pepper, oregano, and ground red pepper in a small bowl. Drain the shrimp and olives, discarding remaining solids. Place the shrimp-and-olive mixture in a jelly-roll pan, and sprinkle with Shrimp Spice Mix.

4. Make the Classic Cocktail Sauce: Stir together the first 5 ingredients in a small bowl until well blended. Add salt and pepper.

5. Make the White Cocktail Sauce: Stir together the first 7 ingredients in a small bowl until well blended. Add salt and pepper.

6. Serve the shrimp immediately with cocktail sauces and lemon wedges, or chill 15 to 20 minutes or until cold.

ROASTED POTATO-AND-OKRA SALAD

This fresh yet hearty side dish features roasted potatoes instead of the boiled ones traditionally served as part of a Lowcountry-style spread.

SERVES 6 to 8 · HANDS-ON: 20 minutes · TOTAL: 1 hour, 40 minutes

ROASTED POTATO-AND-OKRA SALAD:
- 1 pound baby red potatoes
- 1 pound small Yukon Gold potatoes
- 1 pound fresh whole okra
- 2 tablespoons olive oil
- 3 teaspoons kosher salt
- 1 teaspoon freshly ground black pepper

LEMON-THYME VINAIGRETTE:
- 1 small shallot, minced
- 3 tablespoons white wine vinegar
- 1 teaspoon lemon zest
- 2 tablespoons fresh lemon juice
- 1 teaspoon Dijon mustard
- 1 teaspoon chopped fresh thyme
- ¼ cup extra virgin olive oil
- 3 scallions, thinly sliced

Garnish: fresh thyme sprigs

1. Make the salad: Preheat the oven to 450°F. Bring the potatoes and water to cover to a boil in a large saucepan over medium-high. Reduce heat to medium-low, and simmer 15 to 20 minutes or until fork-tender. Drain and cool completely (about 20 minutes).
2. Toss together the okra, 1 tablespoon of the olive oil, 1 teaspoon of the salt, and ½ teaspoon of the pepper, and place in a single layer in a jelly-roll pan. Cut potatoes in half, and toss with remaining olive oil, salt, and pepper. Place potatoes in a single layer in another jelly-roll pan.
3. Bake the okra and potatoes at 450°F for 20 to 25 minutes or until tender and golden brown. Remove from oven, and let stand 5 minutes.
4. Make the vinaigrette: Stir together shallot and white wine vinegar in a small bowl. Let stand 10 minutes. Stir in zest and next 3 ingredients. Add oil in a slow, steady stream, whisking until smooth.
5. Cut the okra pods in half lengthwise. Toss together the potatoes, okra, vinaigrette, and scallions in a medium bowl. Serve immediately.

CRISPY ANDOUILLE HUSH PUPPIES

This crunchy, savory bite is a delicious dockside starter.

SERVES 8 to 10 · HANDS-ON: 20 minutes · TOTAL: 35 minutes

- Vegetable oil
- 1½ cups self-rising white cornmeal mix
- 1 cup diced andouille sausage
- ¾ cup self-rising flour
- ¾ cup finely chopped sweet onion
- 1 large egg, lightly beaten
- ⅔ cup lager beer
- ⅓ cup buttermilk

1. Preheat the oven to 200°F. Pour the oil to a depth of 3 inches into a Dutch oven; heat to 375°F. Stir together the cornmeal and next 3 ingredients in a large bowl. Add the egg, beer, and buttermilk; stir just until moistened. Let stand 10 minutes.
2. Using a 1-inch cookie scoop, drop the batter into hot oil, and fry, in batches, 2 to 3 minutes on each side or until golden brown. Drain on a wire rack over paper towels. Keep warm in a 200°F oven.

BOOZY SHORTCAKES WITH SWEET CREAM

A spirited dessert that celebrates the South's favorite stone fruit.

SERVES 6 · **HANDS-ON:** 20 minutes · **TOTAL:** 1 hour, 35 minutes

6 fresh peaches, sliced
⅓ cup peach schnapps
2 tablespoons fresh lime juice
1 teaspoon vanilla extract
1 tablespoon granulated sugar

¼ cup loosely packed fresh mint leaves, torn
Pinch of kosher salt
1 cup heavy cream
1 tablespoon powdered sugar

6 refrigerated jumbo biscuits (from a 16.3-ounce can)
1 large egg, lightly beaten
3 teaspoons demerara sugar
Garnish: fresh mint sprigs

1. Stir together the first 7 ingredients in a bowl. Cover and let stand 1 hour, stirring occasionally.

2. Beat the heavy cream at medium-high speed with an electric mixer until foamy; gradually add powdered sugar, beating until soft peaks form. Cover and chill until ready to use.

3. Place the biscuits on a baking sheet, and brush with egg. Sprinkle the demerara sugar over biscuits, and bake according to package directions.

4. Split the biscuits, and place bottom halves on individual plates. Spoon the whipped cream over each biscuit, and top with peach slices and remaining biscuit half. Serve immediately.

SHOOFLY PUNCH

*Don't even think of substituting ginger beer's weaker cousin, ginger ale,
in this recipe. The spicy ginger tang is the secret to this cocktail.*

SERVES 6 · HANDS-ON: 15 minutes · TOTAL: 1 hour, 15 minutes, including Simple Syrup

2   cups (16 ounces) bourbon
⅔   cup Domaine de Canton
    Ginger Liqueur
⅔   cup fresh lemon juice

⅔   cup Simple Syrup (page F34)
1½ teaspoons bitters
    Crushed ice

2   cups nonalcoholic ginger
    beer, chilled
6   orange slices
6   mint sprigs

Stir together the first 5 ingredients. Fill 6 glasses or Mason jars with crushed ice. Pour the bourbon
mixture over ice; top with the ginger beer (about ⅓ cup). Add an orange slice and a mint sprig to
each glass. Serve immediately.

NOTE: If you have trouble finding ginger beer, try two Southern ginger ales that can't be beat:
Blenheim's (from South Carolina) or Buffalo Rock (from Alabama).

BACKYARD BBQ

These simple, savory Southern classics are perfect for a backyard celebration.

Menu

Simply Deviled Eggs

Shout Hallelujah Potato Salad

Central Texas Slaw

The Ultimate Smoky, Sweet Ribs

SIMPLY DEVILED EGGS

Try the innovative stir-ins below to make your own signature deviled eggs.
Prepare recipe as directed, stirring one of the following delicious combos into the yolk mixture.

MAKES 2 dozen • **HANDS-ON:** 25 minutes • **TOTAL:** 40 minutes

12 large eggs
⅓ cup fat-free Greek yogurt
2 ounces ⅓-less-fat cream cheese

1 tablespoon chopped fresh parsley
1 teaspoon Dijon mustard

⅛ teaspoon table salt

1. Place the eggs in a single layer in a stainless steel saucepan. (Do not use nonstick.) Add water to a depth of 3 inches. Bring to a rolling boil; cook 1 minute. Cover, remove from heat, and let stand 10 minutes. Drain.

2. Place the eggs under cold running water until just cool enough to handle. Tap the eggs on the counter until cracks form; peel.

3. Slice the eggs in half lengthwise; carefully remove yolks. Mash together the yolks, yogurt and next 4 ingredients until smooth using a fork. Spoon the yolk mixture into egg white halves. Serve immediately, or cover and chill 1 hour before serving.

5 Deviled Egg Favorites

1. CREOLE SHRIMP: ½ cup finely chopped cooked shrimp, 3 tablespoons sautéed chopped green bell pepper, 1 minced scallion, ¼ teaspoon Creole seasoning, ¼ teaspoon hot sauce. Top with cooked shrimp.

2. TEXAS CAVIAR: 3 tablespoons chopped roasted red bell pepper, 1 minced scallion, 1 tablespoon minced pickled jalapeño pepper, 1 tablespoon chopped fresh cilantro, 1 teaspoon Italian dressing mix. Top with canned black-eyed peas and fresh cilantro leaves.

3. HIGH SOCIETY: ½ cup cooked fresh lump crabmeat, 2 teaspoons fresh tarragon, ½ teaspoon lemon zest, ¼ teaspoon freshly ground black pepper. Top with cooked fresh crabmeat and watercress.

4. GEORGIA PEACH: 3 tablespoons peach preserves, ¼ cup finely chopped country ham, 1 teaspoon grated Vidalia onion, ½ teaspoon apple cider vinegar, ¼ teaspoon freshly ground black pepper. Top with sliced fresh peaches and chopped toasted pecans.

5. TRIPLE PICKLE: 3 tablespoons chopped sweet pickles, 2 tablespoons chopped capers. Top with pickled okra slices.

SHOUT HALLELUJAH POTATO SALAD

Bragging rights for this flavor-packed, perfectly balanced favorite
(from The Southern Foodways Alliance Community Cookbook) go to Blair Hobbs of Oxford, MS.

SERVES 12 • **HANDS-ON:** 25 minutes • **TOTAL:** 40 minutes

- 5 pounds Yukon Gold potatoes
- 4 large hard-cooked eggs, peeled
- 1 tablespoon table salt
- 1 cup plus 2 tablespoons mayonnaise
- 1 cup sweet salad cube pickles, drained
- ½ cup chopped red onion
- ½ cup chopped green bell pepper
- ½ cup chopped celery
- ¼ cup chopped fresh flat-leaf parsley
- ¼ cup yellow mustard
- 1 (4-ounce) jar diced pimiento, drained
- 2 tablespoons seasoned rice wine vinegar
- 2 tablespoons fresh lemon juice
- 1 tablespoon extra virgin olive oil
- 1 to 2 jalapeño peppers, seeded and minced
- 1 to 2 teaspoons celery salt
- 4 drops of hot sauce
- Freshly ground black pepper
- ½ teaspoon smoked paprika

1. Cook the potatoes in boiling water to cover 20 minutes or until tender; drain and cool 15 minutes. Peel the potatoes, and place in a large bowl. Add the eggs, and chop mixture into bite-size pieces. Sprinkle with the salt; toss to coat.

2. Stir together the mayonnaise and next 14 ingredients; gently stir into potato mixture. Sprinkle with the paprika. Serve immediately, or cover and chill up to 2 days.

CENTRAL TEXAS SLAW

This slaw packs a bit of punch and southwestern flair, thanks to jalapeño pepper and cilantro.

MAKES 4 cups · **HANDS-ON:** 15 minutes · **TOTAL:** 1 hour, 15 minutes

¼ cup white vinegar
¼ cup extra virgin olive oil
2 tablespoons sugar
3 to 4 tablespoons fresh
    lime juice
1½ teaspoons kosher salt
½ teaspoon ground coriander
¼ teaspoon ground cumin

¼ teaspoon ground red pepper
¼ teaspoon freshly ground
    black pepper
2 cups thinly sliced
    red cabbage
2 cups thinly sliced
    green cabbage
½ cup shredded carrot

1 medium jalapeño pepper
    (with seeds), thinly sliced
½ red bell pepper, thinly sliced
½ yellow bell pepper,
    thinly sliced
½ cup chopped fresh cilantro

Whisk together the vinegar, olive oil, sugar, lime juice, kosher salt, ground coriander, ground cumin, ground red pepper, and freshly ground black pepper in a large bowl. Add the red cabbage, green cabbage, carrot, jalapeño pepper, red bell pepper, and yellow bell pepper. Toss to coat. Chill 1 hour before serving, tossing occasionally. Stir in the cilantro just before serving.

Shout Hallelujah
Potato Salad

Central Texas Slaw

THE ULTIMATE SMOKY, SWEET RIBS

For tender, juicy, fall-off-the-bone-good barbecue ribs, fire up your smoker—or grill.

SERVES 4 to 6 · **HANDS-ON:** 45 minutes · **TOTAL:** 15 hours, 10 minutes, including rub, braising liquid, and sauce

RIBS:
- 2 (2½- to 3-pound) slabs St. Louis-style pork ribs

SMOKY DRY RUB:
- ¼ cup firmly packed dark brown sugar
- 2 tablespoons smoked paprika
- 1 tablespoon kosher salt
- 2 teaspoons garlic salt
- 2 teaspoons chili powder
- 2 teaspoons freshly ground black pepper
- 1 teaspoon onion salt
- 1 teaspoon celery salt
- 1 teaspoon ground red pepper
- 1 teaspoon ground cumin
- 1 cup apple wood smoking chips

RIB BRAISING LIQUID:
- 1 cup apple juice
- 1 tablespoon Smoky Dry Rub
- 2 teaspoons balsamic vinegar
- 1 garlic clove, minced

SWEET-AND-SPICY BARBECUE SAUCE:
- ½ cup chopped sweet onion
- 2 garlic cloves, minced
- 1 jalapeño pepper, seeded and minced
- 1 tablespoon olive oil
- 1 (32-ounce) bottle ketchup
- 1 cup firmly packed dark brown sugar
- 1 cup apple cider vinegar
- ½ cup apple juice
- ½ cup honey
- 1 tablespoon Worcestershire sauce
- 1 teaspoon kosher salt
- 1 teaspoon freshly ground black pepper
- 1 teaspoon celery seeds
- ½ teaspoon dried crushed red pepper

1. Make the ribs: Rinse the ribs, and pat dry. Remove thin membrane from back of each slab by slicing into it and pulling it off. (This will make the ribs more tender.)

2. Make the rub: Stir together the brown sugar and next 9 ingredients. Rub both sides of ribs with the Smoky Dry Rub (about 3 to 4 tablespoons per slab), pressing gently to adhere. Wrap each slab in plastic wrap, and chill 8 to 12 hours.

3. Soak wood chips in water 30 minutes. Prepare smoker according to manufacturer's directions, bringing internal temperature to 225° to 250°F; maintain temperature 15 to 20 minutes.

4. Drain wood chips, and place on coals. Remove the ribs from plastic wrap, and place ribs, meat side up, on cooking grate; cover with smoker lid.

5. Smoke the ribs, maintaining temperature inside smoker between 225° and 250°F for 3½ hours.

6. Make the braising liquid: Stir together the apple juice and next 3 ingredients. Remove the ribs from smoker. Place each slab, meat side down, on a large piece of heavy-duty aluminum foil. (Foil should be large enough to completely wrap slab.) Bring up edges of foil to contain liquid. Pour half of the Rib Braising Liquid over each slab. Tightly wrap each slab in foil. Return the slabs, meat side down, to smoker. Cook, covered with lid, 1 to 1½ hours, checking for tenderness after 1 hour.

7. Make the sauce: Sauté the onion, garlic, and jalapeño pepper in hot olive oil in a large saucepan over medium-high 4 to 5 minutes or until tender. Stir in the ketchup and next 9 ingredients. Bring to a boil, stirring occasionally. Reduce heat to low; simmer, stirring occasionally, 30 minutes. Remove the ribs; unwrap and discard foil. Generously brush both sides of the slabs with the Sweet-and-Spicy Barbecue Sauce. Return the ribs to smoker, and smoke 20 minutes or until caramelized.

BRIDAL SHOWER BRUNCH

Bring out the fine linen, polish the silver, and go wild with bouquets for a pretty outdoor brunch the bride will never forget.

Menu

Judy's Bloody Mary Mix

BLT Benedict with Avocado-Tomato Relish

Tipsy Red-and-Yellow Watermelon Salad

Strawberry Shortcake

JUDY'S BLOODY MARY MIX

A Bloody Mary bar lets guests make their own signature sip.

MAKES about 2 quarts • HANDS-ON: 5 minutes • TOTAL: 5 minutes, plus chill time

6 **cups tomato juice**
1¼ **cups lime juice**
½ **cup Worcestershire sauce**

4 **dashes hot sauce (such as Tabasco)**
1 **tablespoon kosher salt**

1 **tablespoon prepared horseradish**
Cracked pepper

Stir together the first 6 ingredients. Add cracked pepper to taste. Refrigerate in an airtight container for 3 days.

NOTE: Make this Bloody Mary mix at least 3 days prior to serving.

BLT BENEDICT WITH AVOCADO-TOMATO RELISH

Immediately after poaching, place eggs in ice water, and refrigerate until serving time.
Drain eggs; place in boiling water 45 seconds, and drain again. Serve immediately.

SERVES 6 · HANDS-ON: 15 minutes · TOTAL: 15 minutes

- 1 cup halved grape tomatoes
- 1 avocado, diced
- 1 tablespoon chopped fresh basil
- 1 garlic clove, minced
- 2 tablespoons extra virgin olive oil
- Salt and pepper
- 1 tablespoon red wine vinegar
- 6 large eggs
- ¼ cup mayonnaise
- 6 (¾-inch-thick) bakery bread slices, toasted
- 3 cups firmly packed arugula
- 12 thick bacon slices, cooked

1. Combine tomatoes, next 4 ingredients, table salt and black pepper to taste, and 2½ teaspoons of the red wine vinegar in a small bowl.

2. Add water to depth of 3 inches in a large saucepan. Bring to a boil; reduce heat, and maintain at a light simmer. Add remaining ½ teaspoon red wine vinegar. Break eggs, 1 at a time, and slip into water, as close as possible to surface. Simmer 3 to 5 minutes or to desired degree of doneness. Remove with a slotted spoon. Trim edges, if desired.

3. Spread mayonnaise on 1 side of each bread slice. Layer each with ½ cup arugula, 2 bacon slices, and 1 egg. Top with tomato mixture.

TIPSY RED-AND-YELLOW WATERMELON SALAD

Try this with honeydew and cantaloupe, too, for a change of flavor and color.

SERVES 6 to 8 · HANDS-ON: 20 minutes · TOTAL: 1 hour, 20 minutes

½ (6-pound) red watermelon
½ (6-pound) yellow watermelon
1 cup fresh lemon juice (about 10 to 12 lemons)

⅔ cup sugar
½ cup vodka
⅓ cup black raspberry liqueur
Pinch of fine sea salt

1 tablespoon chopped fresh mint

1. Scoop watermelons into balls using various-size melon ballers, and place watermelon in a large bowl.

2. Whisk together lemon juice and next 4 ingredients in a medium bowl until sugar dissolves. Pour lemon juice mixture over watermelon balls; gently stir to coat. Cover and chill 1 to 2 hours.

3. Gently toss watermelon balls. Sprinkle salad with chopped fresh mint. Serve immediately with a slotted spoon.

STRAWBERRY SHORTCAKE

The shortcake layers can be baked earlier in the day. Plan ahead for slicing and chilling the strawberries. Assemble cake with whipped cream just before serving.

SERVES 8 · HANDS-ON: 30 minutes · TOTAL: 2 hours, 8 minutes

2 (16-ounce) containers fresh strawberries, sliced
¼ to ½ cup granulated sugar
½ cup butter, softened and divided
2 cups all-purpose flour
1 tablespoon plus 1 teaspoon baking powder
¼ teaspoon table salt
¼ cup granulated sugar
Dash of ground nutmeg
½ cup milk
2 large eggs, separated
¼ cup granulated sugar
1 cup heavy cream
¼ cup powdered sugar

1. Combine sliced strawberries and desired amount of granulated sugar; stir gently, and chill 1 to 2 hours. Drain.

2. Preheat oven to 450°F. Butter 2 (9-inch) round cake pans with ½ teaspoon butter each. Combine flour and next 4 ingredients in a large bowl; cut in remaining butter with a pastry blender until mixture is crumbly.

3. Whisk together milk and egg yolks. Add to flour mixture; stir with a fork until a soft dough forms. Pat dough out into prepared cake pans. (Dough will be sticky; moisten fingers with water as necessary.)

4. Beat egg whites at medium speed with an electric mixer just until stiff peaks form. Brush surface of dough with beaten egg white; sprinkle with ¼ cup granulated sugar.

5. Bake at 450°F for 8 to 10 minutes or until layers are golden brown. (Layers will be thin.) Remove from pans to wire racks, and let cool completely (about 30 minutes).

6. Beat heavy cream until foamy; gradually add powdered sugar, beating until soft peaks form. Place 1 cake layer on a serving plate. Spread half of whipped cream over layer, and arrange half of sweetened strawberries on top. Repeat procedure with remaining layer, whipped cream, and sweetened strawberries, reserving a small amount of whipped cream. Top cake with remaining whipped cream. Store any leftovers in refrigerator.

GAME DAY GATHERING

Whether you're tailgate bound or couch-lounging, tasty fortification is a requirement for any championship get-together.

Menu

Georgia-Style Boiled Peanuts

Baked Pimiento Cheese Dip

Asian-Ginger Wings with Lime-Cilantro Ranch Dip

Chipotle-Barbecue Meatballs

Game Day Sheet Cake

Georgia-Style Boiled Peanuts

GEORGIA-STYLE BOILED PEANUTS

Boiled peanuts are easily made in a slow cooker. You can start them before bed and have them ready for tailgating the next afternoon.

MAKES 18 cups · **HANDS-ON:** 5 minutes · **TOTAL:** 18 hours, 5 minutes

2 pounds raw peanuts, in shell	¾ cup table salt	12 cups water

Combine all ingredients in a 5- or 6-quart slow cooker. Cover and cook on HIGH 18 hours or until peanuts are soft. Drain the peanuts before serving or storing. Refrigerate the peanuts in zip-top plastic freezer bags up to 2 weeks.

BAKED PIMIENTO CHEESE DIP

This irresistibly cheesy dip is great with celery sticks or crackers or even as a topping for baked potatoes, open-faced tomato sandwiches, or hot brown sandwiches.

MAKES 5 cups · **HANDS-ON:** 17 minutes · **TOTAL:** 2 Hours

1 (10-ounce) block sharp Cheddar cheese, shredded	8 bacon slices, cooked and crumbled	2 (4-ounce) jars diced pimiento, drained
1 (10-ounce) block extra-sharp Cheddar cheese, shredded	½ small onion, finely grated	2 teaspoons Worcestershire sauce
1 tablespoon cornstarch	1 cup mayonnaise	¼ teaspoon black pepper

1. Toss together cheeses and cornstarch in a medium bowl. Add half of bacon, onion, and remaining ingredients; stir well to blend. Spoon mixture into a lightly greased 3-quart slow cooker. Sprinkle with remaining half of bacon.

2. Cover and cook on LOW 2 to 3 hours or until melted and bubbly. Serve warm with crackers.

NOTE: We tested with Cracker Barrel Sharp and Extra Sharp Cheddar cheeses.

TIP: The addition of cornstarch to classic pimiento cheese helps to keep the oil from separating when the dip is heated. You may want to give the dip a quick stir before serving.

ASIAN-GINGER WINGS

Wings and football are like baseball and hot dogs. This recipe may become your new favorite.

SERVES 4 • **HANDS-ON:** 15 minutes • **TOTAL:** 4 hours, 15 minutes, not including dip

4 pounds chicken wing pieces (about 32 wings)
¼ cup honey
1 cup garlic-green onion teriyaki sauce

2 tablespoons grated fresh ginger
3 tablespoons fresh lime juice
½ teaspoon lime zest
3 cloves garlic, sliced

Lime-Cilantro Ranch Dip
Garnishes: sesame seeds, sliced scallions, sliced red chile peppers

1. Preheat the broiler with the oven rack 3 inches from heat. Place the wings on a lightly greased rack in a lightly greased broiler pan.

2. Broil 14 minutes or until browned. Transfer the wings to a lightly greased 5-quart slow cooker.

3. Stir together the honey, teriyaki sauce, ginger, lime juice, lime zest, and garlic in a small bowl. Pour the honey mixture over wings. Cover and cook on LOW 4 hours.

NOTE: We tested with Kikkoman Teriyaki Garlic & Green Onion Sauce.

Lime-Cilantro Ranch Dip

MAKES about 1½ cups • **HANDS-ON:** 5 minutes • **TOTAL:** 35 minutes

1 (1-ounce) envelope Ranch dressing mix
1½ cups light sour cream

1 tablespoon fresh lime juice
1 tablespoon chopped cilantro

Quesadillas, tacos, or chili (optional)

Whisk together the first 4 ingredients. Cover and chill 30 minutes. Serve as a dipping sauce for these zesty wings or as a creamy accent on quesadillas, tacos, or chili.

CHIPOTLE-BARBECUE MEATBALLS

Chipotles are smoky jalapeños in zesty adobo sauce. They give these meatballs grilled flavor without a fire.

SERVES 12 to 14 as an appetizer · **HANDS-ON:** 10 minutes · **TOTAL:** 50 minutes

1 (28-ounce) bottle barbecue sauce

1 (18-ounce) jar cherry preserves

3 canned chipotle peppers in adobo sauce

1 tablespoon adobo sauce from can

2 (16-ounce) packages frozen meatballs

Garnish: chopped fresh chives

Whisk together first 4 ingredients and 1½ cups water in a Dutch oven. Bring to a boil over medium-high. Add meatballs; return to a boil. Reduce heat to medium, and simmer, stirring occasionally, 40 to 45 minutes. (Sauce will thicken.) Keep warm in a slow cooker on WARM or LOW, if desired.

GAME DAY SHEET CAKE

Bake one for the team! With our icing colors, you can show spirit in every slice.

SERVES 12 to 15 • **HANDS-ON:** 20 minutes • **TOTAL:** 2 hours, 15 minutes

1¼ cups butter, softened
2¼ cups sugar
7 large egg whites, at room temperature

3½ cups cake flour
4 teaspoons baking powder
1 cup water

1 tablespoon vanilla extract
Vanilla Buttercream Frosting

1. Preheat oven to 325°F. Lightly grease and flour a 13- x 9-inch pan. Beat butter and sugar at medium speed with a heavy-duty electric stand mixer until fluffy. Gradually add egg whites, one-third at a time, beating well after each addition.

2. Sift together cake flour and baking powder; gradually add to butter mixture alternately with 1 cup water, beginning and ending with flour mixture. Stir in vanilla. Pour batter into the prepared pan.

3. Bake at 325°F for 45 to 50 minutes or until a wooden pick inserted in center comes out clean. Cool completely in pan on a wire rack (about 1 hour). Remove from pan to a serving platter. Spread top and sides of cake with frosting.

Vanilla Buttercream Frosting

Customize the icing with your team colors (see frosting formulas below).

MAKES about 5 cups · **HANDS-ON:** 10 minutes · **TOTAL:** 10 minutes

1 cup butter, softened
½ cup milk

1 tablespoon vanilla extract

2 (16-ounce) packages powdered sugar

Beat butter at medium speed with an electric mixer until creamy. Stir together milk and vanilla. Gradually add powdered sugar to butter mixture alternately with milk mixture, beating at low speed just until blended after each addition and scraping down sides of bowl as needed.

Icing Color Formulas for Sheet Cake

Recipes are for 1 cup Vanilla Buttercream Frosting. One drop is the size of a 4 mm round nail head. Gel paste will thicken after bottles are opened. If your gel paste comes out in drops larger than the 4 mm round nail head, count 1 large drop as 3 drops. We tested with AmeriColor Soft Gel Paste colors (from $1.35/color for a ¾-ounce bottle). Because our formulas were tested with AmeriColor, we suggest using their products for results equal to our own. For a list of retailers, visit americolorcorp.com.

GEORGIA
¾ teaspoon plus 8 drops Red Red
8 drops Burgundy
8 drops Maroon

ALABAMA
¼ teaspoon Super Red
8 drops Maroon
4 drops Regal Purple

TEXAS A&M
¼ teaspoon Maroon

FLORIDA STATE
¼ teaspoon Maroon
8 drops Warm Brown
8 drops Regal Purple

WEST VIRGINIA
¼ teaspoon plus ⅛ teaspoon plus 4 drops Navy Blue
5 drops Super Black

APPALACHIAN STATE
10 drops Electric Yellow
5 drops Gold
2 drops Bright White

TEXAS
⅛ teaspoon Orange
2 drops Maroon
1 drop Lemon Yellow

OKLAHOMA STATE
¼ teaspoon plus ⅛ teaspoon plus 4 drops Terra-cotta
⅛ teaspoon plus 4 drops Lemon Yellow
8 drops Warm Brown

MARSHALL
⅛ teaspoon Leaf Green
5 drops Forest Green
1 drop Super Black

VANDERBILT
⅛ teaspoon plus 4 drops Warm Brown
8 drops Avocado
8 drops Lemon Yellow
Wilton Gold Sparkle Gel on top

TENNESSEE
¼ teaspoon plus 4 drops Orange

LOUISIANA
¼ teaspoon plus 8 drops Egg Yellow

CLEMSON
⅛ teaspoon plus 8 drops Regal Purple
2 drops Super Black

VIRGINIA TECH
⅛ teaspoon plus 2 drops Orange
5 drops Red Red

PUMPKIN PATCH BASH

From pumpkin patch to pot, pan, and pie plate, we celebrate this cool-weather squash.

Menu

Spicy Pumpkin Soup with Avocado Cream

Pear-and-Pumpkin Tart

Pumpkin-and-Turnip Green Lasagna

Pumpkin-Chocolate Brownies

Pumpkin Pie

SPICY PUMPKIN SOUP WITH AVOCADO CREAM

If you don't have any buttermilk for the avocado cream sauce, substitute plain yogurt and just a little water.

SERVES 6 to 8 · HANDS-ON: 55 minutes · TOTAL: 55 minutes

1 cup diced yellow onion
3 tablespoons olive oil
1½ teaspoons kosher salt
2 garlic cloves, chopped
1 tablespoon ground cumin
1 (29-ounce) can pumpkin
6 to 6½ cups reduced-sodium chicken broth
1 canned chipotle pepper in adobo sauce

1 tablespoon adobo sauce from can
1 medium avocado, peeled and diced
½ cup whole buttermilk
2 tablespoons fresh lime juice
2 tablespoons extra virgin olive oil
¼ cup water

8 ounces smoked sausage, sliced
1 cup black beans, drained and rinsed
½ teaspoon smoked paprika
Garnish: cilantro sprigs

1. Place the onions, 2 tablespoons of the olive oil, and 1 teaspoon of the salt in a Dutch oven over medium; cook, covered, 5 to 6 minutes or until translucent. Stir in the garlic and cumin; cook 2 minutes. Whisk in the pumpkin and 6 cups of the broth; add chipotle pepper and 1 tablespoon adobo sauce. Increase heat to medium-high, and simmer, stirring occasionally, 12 minutes.

2. Process the soup, in batches, in a food processor or blender 1 minute. Add up to ½ cup remaining broth, 2 tablespoons at a time, to reach desired consistency.

3. Process the avocado, next 3 ingredients, and remaining ½ teaspoon salt in a blender until smooth. Add up to ¼ cup water, 1 tablespoon at a time, to reach desired consistency.

4. Cook the smoked sausage in remaining 1 tablespoon olive oil in a large skillet over medium, stirring occasionally, 3 minutes. Stir in the black beans and paprika, and cook 1 minute. Ladle the soup into serving bowls; top with sausage mixture and avocado cream.

PEAR-AND-PUMPKIN TART

Need help peeling and cutting your pumpkin?
Most supermarket produce sections offer this service for a small fee.

MAKES 6 to 8 appetizer servings · HANDS-ON: 20 minutes · TOTAL: 50 minutes

1 (17.3-ounce) package frozen puff pastry sheets, thawed
½ (3-pound) sugar pumpkin, peeled, seeded, and cut into ¼-inch-thick slices
1 firm Bartlett pear, cut into ¼-inch-thick slices
½ teaspoon kosher salt
¼ teaspoon freshly ground black pepper
2 teaspoons olive oil
2 cups loosely packed arugula leaves
¼ cup crumbled blue cheese
¼ cup fresh pomegranate seeds
1 teaspoon red wine vinegar

1. Preheat the oven to 425°F. Unfold the puff pastry sheets, and place side by side on a baking sheet, overlapping short sides ½ inch. Press seam to seal. Score a ½-inch border on all sides, using a knife. Do not cut through pastry.

2. Toss together the pumpkin slices, next 3 ingredients, and 1 teaspoon of the olive oil in a large bowl. Spread the mixture in a single layer on prepared pastry sheets, leaving a ½-inch border.

3. Bake at 425°F for 20 to 22 minutes or until pastry is golden brown. Cool on a wire rack 10 minutes.

4. Toss together the arugula, next 3 ingredients, and remaining 1 teaspoon olive oil in a medium bowl. Add salt and pepper to taste. Sprinkle the mixture over the tart, and cut into desired shapes.

PUMPKIN-AND-TURNIP GREEN LASAGNA

Use no-boil noodles (we like Barilla brand), which will soak up the sauce and pumpkin.

SERVES 6 to 8 · HANDS-ON: 1 hour · TOTAL: 1 hour, 55 minutes

Vegetable cooking spray
1 pound mild Italian sausage, casings removed
2 tablespoons olive oil
2 garlic cloves, finely chopped
2½ teaspoons kosher salt
1 (1-pound) package fresh turnip greens, chopped
½ cup water

1½ quarts milk
3 ounces (6 tablespoons) butter
6 tablespoons all-purpose flour
½ teaspoon dry mustard
8 ounces shredded Parmesan cheese (2 cups)

¾ teaspoon freshly ground black pepper
½ teaspoon ground nutmeg
1 (29-ounce) can pumpkin
1 pound no-boil lasagna noodles
Freshly grated Parmesan cheese

1. Preheat the oven to 375°F. Lightly grease a 13- x 9-inch baking dish with cooking spray. Cook the sausage in 1 tablespoon of the olive oil in a large skillet over medium-high, stirring often, 4 to 5 minutes or until meat crumbles and is no longer pink. Remove the sausage to a plate, using a slotted spoon; reserve drippings in skillet. Reduce heat to medium.

2. Stir the garlic, ½ teaspoon of the salt, half of turnip greens, ½ cup water, and remaining 1 tablespoon oil into hot drippings. Cook 1 minute, stirring to loosen browned bits from bottom of skillet. Stir in remaining turnip greens. Reduce heat to medium-low, and cook 5 to 6 minutes or until greens are tender and water has evaporated. Remove from heat.

3. Microwave the milk, in batches, in a microwave-safe measuring cup covered with plastic wrap at HIGH for 2 to 3 minutes or until very warm. Melt the butter in a large saucepan over medium. Whisk in the flour, and cook, whisking constantly, 1 minute. Gradually whisk in the warm milk; cook, whisking often, 12 to 14 minutes or until mixture thickens and comes to a low boil. Remove from heat, and whisk in the dry mustard, 1 cup of the Parmesan cheese, ¼ teaspoon of the pepper, ¼ teaspoon of the nutmeg, and 1 teaspoon of the salt.

4. Whisk together the pumpkin, ¾ cup of the Parmesan cheese, remaining ¼ teaspoon ground nutmeg, remaining 1 teaspoon salt, and remaining ½ teaspoon pepper in a large bowl.

5. Place 1 layer of lasagna noodles in prepared baking dish, covering bottom completely. (Use pieces of noodles to fill in any gaps.) Spread 1 cup sauce over noodles; top with cooked sausage. Add another layer of noodles and 1 cup sauce; top with half of pumpkin mixture. Add another layer of noodles and 1 cup sauce; top with turnip green mixture. Add another layer of noodles and 1 cup sauce; top with remaining pumpkin mixture. Add another layer of noodles and 1 cup sauce; top with remaining ¼ cup Parmesan cheese.

6. Bake at 375°F for 40 minutes or until top is golden brown. Let stand 15 minutes before serving. Sprinkle with the freshly grated Parmesan cheese. Serve with remaining sauce.

PUMPKIN-CHOCOLATE BROWNIES

For a perfect slice, cut while they're cold. Serve at room temperature.

MAKES 24 · HANDS-ON: 40 minutes · TOTAL: 4 hours, 5 minutes

Butter

Parchment paper

1¼ cups semisweet chocolate morsels

8 ounces (1 cup) unsalted butter, cut into pieces

3 (1-ounce) unsweetened chocolate baking squares, chopped

3 large eggs

1 cup plus 2 tablespoons granulated sugar

2 tablespoons cold brewed coffee

1 tablespoon vanilla extract

⅔ cup (3 ounces) all-purpose flour

1½ teaspoons baking powder

1 teaspoon kosher salt

1 (15-ounce) can pumpkin

3 large eggs

½ cup heavy cream

⅓ cup firmly packed light brown sugar

1½ teaspoons pumpkin pie spice

1. Preheat the oven to 350°F. Grease a 13- x 9-inch baking pan with butter. Line bottom and sides of pan with parchment paper, allowing 2 to 3 inches to extend over sides. Grease (with butter) and flour parchment paper. Pour water to a depth of 1 inch in the bottom of a double boiler over medium; bring to a boil. Reduce heat, and simmer. Place the chocolate morsels and next 2 ingredients in top of double boiler over simmering water. Cook, stirring occasionally, 5 to 6 minutes or until melted. Remove from heat; cool 10 minutes.

2. Whisk together the 3 eggs, granulated sugar, and next 2 ingredients in a large bowl. Gradually whisk the warm chocolate mixture into the egg mixture; cool 10 minutes.

3. Sift together the flour, baking powder, and ½ teaspoon of the salt in a bowl. Whisk into the cooled chocolate mixture. Pour the batter into prepared pan, reserving ⅔ cup.

4. Whisk together the pumpkin, next 4 ingredients, and remaining ½ teaspoon salt; pour over brownie batter in pan. Top with the reserved brownie batter, and swirl batter gently 3 times in 1 direction and 3 times in the opposite direction with a knife or the end of a wooden spoon.

5. Bake at 350°F for 45 to 50 minutes or until a wooden pick inserted in center comes out with a few moist crumbs. Cool completely on a wire rack (about 2 hours). Lift the brownies from pan, using parchment paper sides as handles. Gently remove parchment paper, and cut brownies into 24 squares.

PUMPKIN PIE

For a crisp crust, use a metal pie pan and prebake the crust with pie weights.

SERVES 8 · HANDS-ON: 15 minutes · TOTAL: 2 hours, 15 minutes

1 (14.1-ounce) package refrigerated piecrusts
1½ cups plus 2 tablespoons buttermilk

Parchment paper
1 (15-ounce) can pumpkin
¾ cup sugar
2 teaspoons ground cinnamon

½ teaspoon kosher salt
1 teaspoon vanilla extract
2 large eggs
1 large egg yolk

1. Preheat the oven to 425°F. Fit 1 piecrust into a 9-inch metal pie pan according to package directions, pressing excess dough onto rim of pie pan. Cut the shapes from remaining piecrust to use around pie edge. (We used a ½-inch round cutter.) Brush 1 tablespoon of the buttermilk around pie edge; arrange shapes around pie edge, pressing to adhere. Brush the shapes with 1 tablespoon of the buttermilk. Prick bottom and sides of piecrust 8 to 10 times with a fork. Line the piecrust with parchment paper, and fill with pie weights. Bake at 425°F for 15 minutes.

2. Whisk together the pumpkin, next 6 ingredients, and remaining 1½ cups buttermilk in a large bowl. Pour the mixture into piecrust.

3. Bake at 425°F for 10 minutes. Reduce oven temperature to 325°F, and bake at 325°F for 35 to 40 more minutes or until edge of filling is slightly puffed and center is slightly jiggly. Cool on a wire rack 1 hour. Store in refrigerator up to 2 days.

MAKE-AHEAD THANKSGIVING

Say "good-bye" to the stress of holiday entertaining and "hello" to a happy host.

Menu

Dry-Brined-and-Marinated Smoked Turkey

Roasted Vegetable Salad with Apple Cider Vinaigrette

Potatoes with Greens

Parsnip-Potato Soup

Cornbread Dressing

Easy Butter Rolls

Pumpkin-Espresso Tiramisù

DRY-BRINED-AND-MARINATED SMOKED TURKEY

Dry-brine the turkey two days before Thanksgiving, and smoke it the day before. Cut the turkey into pieces (legs, breast, wings, etc.), and place in a zip-top plastic freezer bag. Store in the refrigerator. About an hour before dinner, place turkey pieces in a single layer on a baking sheet, and cover with aluminum foil. Warm in a 300°F oven until heated.

SERVES 10 to 12 • **HANDS-ON:** 30 minutes • **TOTAL:** 15 hours, 40 minutes, including dry rub

1 **(12- to 14-pound) whole fresh or frozen, thawed, turkey**

TURKEY DRY RUB:
2 **tablespoons kosher salt**
2 **tablespoons dark brown sugar**

2 **teaspoons freshly ground black pepper**
2 **teaspoons smoked paprika**
½ **teaspoon garlic powder**

MARINADE:
1 **cup apple cider**
2 **tablespoons dark brown sugar**
1 **tablespoon kosher salt**

3 **cups hickory wood chips, soaked in water**

1. Pat the turkey dry with paper towels.

2. Make the rub: Stir together kosher salt and next 4 ingredients. Reserve 2 tablespoons Turkey Dry Rub; sprinkle remaining dry rub over entire turkey, rubbing into skin. Chill turkey 10 to 24 hours.

3. Prepare smoker according to manufacturer's instructions, bringing internal temperature to 250° to 260°F; maintain temperature 15 to 20 minutes.

4. Make the marinade: Stir together apple cider, 2 tablespoons brown sugar, 1 tablespoon salt, and reserved 2 tablespoons Turkey Dry Rub. Attach needle to marinade injector, and fill with cider mixture according to package directions. Inject the top of turkey, thighs, and legs at 1-inch intervals with the cider mixture. Add wood chips to coals, and smoke turkey, maintaining temperature inside smoker between 250° and 260°F, for 5 to 6 hours or until a meat thermometer inserted into thickest portion registers 160°F.

5. Remove turkey, cover loosely with aluminum foil; let stand 10 to 15 minutes before slicing.

ROASTED VEGETABLE SALAD WITH APPLE CIDER VINAIGRETTE

Store roasted vegetables in a zip-top plastic freezer bag or an airtight container in the fridge. Before serving, return to room temperature and add the vinaigrette.

SERVES 8 to 10 • **HANDS-ON:** 30 minutes • **TOTAL:** 3 hours, 15 minutes, including vinaigrette

ROASTED VEGETABLE SALAD:
- 1 pound parsnips, peeled and cut lengthwise
- 1 pound carrots, peeled and cut lengthwise
- 1 pound small golden beets, peeled and coarsely chopped
- 10 to 12 garlic cloves
- 1 cup frozen pearl onions, thawed
- 1 pound small Brussels sprouts, trimmed and halved
- 3 fresh rosemary or thyme sprigs
- 3 small bay leaves
- 1½ ounces (3 tablespoons) butter, melted
- 1½ tablespoons olive oil
- Kosher salt
- Freshly ground black pepper

APPLE CIDER VINAIGRETTE:
- ¾ cup extra virgin olive oil
- ¼ cup apple cider
- ¼ cup apple cider vinegar
- 2 tablespoons finely chopped shallot
- 1 tablespoon whole-grain Dijon mustard
- 1 tablespoon honey
- 1½ teaspoons kosher salt
- 1 teaspoon fresh thyme leaves
- ½ teaspoon freshly ground black pepper
- 1 head radicchio, separated into leaves

1. Make the salad: Preheat the oven to 425°F. Line 2 jelly-roll pans with aluminum foil. Divide the first 8 ingredients between prepared pans. Drizzle with the butter and oil; toss to coat. Spread the vegetables in a single layer in each pan, leaving about 1 inch between pieces. Add salt and pepper to taste.

2. Bake both pans at 425°F at the same time for 20 minutes, placing 1 pan on middle oven rack and 1 pan on lower oven rack. Rotate pans front to back and top rack to bottom rack. Bake at 425°F for 20 to 25 more minutes or until vegetables are tender.

3. Gently loosen the vegetables, and add salt and pepper. Cool completely (about 20 minutes). Discard the herb sprigs and bay leaves. Place the vegetables in a zip-top plastic freezer bag, and refrigerate 2 hours to 3 days.

4. Make the vinaigrette: Combine oil and next 8 ingredients in a glass jar with a tight-fitting lid. Cover with lid, and shake well.

5. To serve, let vegetables stand 20 minutes or until room temperature. Add ¼ cup vinaigrette; toss to coat. Arrange radicchio leaves on a serving platter; top with roasted vegetables. Drizzle ¼ cup vinaigrette over salad. Add salt and pepper to taste. Serve salad with remaining vinaigrette.

NOTE: Store vinaigrette, covered, in the fridge. Let stand 10 minutes or until room temperature. Shake well, and check seasoning before using.

POTATOES WITH GREENS

Prepare this recipe through Step 4, and freeze. Thaw potato mixture in the fridge at least 24 hours before you plan to serve, and let it stand 20 minutes before baking as directed.

SERVES 8 to 10 • **HANDS-ON:** 30 minutes • **TOTAL:** 9 hours, 30 minutes

Butter

4   ounces (½ cup) butter, softened and divided

6   cups shredded kale, chard, cabbage, or other leafy greens

½   cup thinly sliced scallions, white and light green parts only

¼   cup reduced-sodium chicken broth

Kosher salt

Freshly ground black pepper

4   pounds small russet or Yukon Gold potatoes, peeled and cut into 2-inch pieces

1   tablespoon kosher salt

4   ounces cream cheese, softened

1   cup milk

1. Grease a 2½-quart gratin dish or baking dish with butter. Melt 2 tablespoons of the softened butter in a large stockpot over medium-high. Add the kale and green scallions; stir to coat. Add the broth; cover and cook, stirring often, 10 minutes or until vegetables are tender. Add salt and pepper to taste. Transfer to a bowl; cover to keep warm.

2. Bring the potatoes, 1 tablespoon salt, and water to cover to a boil in stockpot over high. Reduce heat to medium, and simmer 20 minutes or just until potatoes are tender. Drain the potatoes, and let stand 3 minutes or until dry. Return to stockpot. Mash with a potato masher until smooth; stir in the cream cheese and 4 tablespoons of the butter. Fold in the kale mixture.

3. Microwave the milk in a microwave-safe measuring cup at HIGH 1 to 2 minutes or until warm. Stir ½ cup of the warm milk into potato mixture. Add up to ½ cup more milk, 1 tablespoon at a time, and stir until mixture thickens. (Mixture will firm up as it chills in Step 4.) Add salt and pepper to taste.

4. Transfer the mixture to prepared dish. Dot with remaining 2 tablespoons butter. Cover dish tightly with plastic wrap, and then with aluminum foil. Chill 8 hours to 5 days, or freeze up to 2 weeks.

5. Preheat the oven to 350°F. Remove plastic wrap and foil from casserole, and let it stand 20 minutes. Bake at 350°F for 30 minutes or until thoroughly heated. Serve warm.

PARSNIP-POTATO SOUP

Make Ahead: Once it's cooled, freeze this silky soup in zip-top plastic freezer bags. Thaw in the refrigerator three to four days before using. Reheat over medium-low. Add table salt and freshly ground black pepper if needed, and garnish just before serving.

MAKES about 2½ quarts · **HANDS-ON:** 50 minutes · **TOTAL:** 1 hour, 5 minutes

3 leeks
1½ ounces (3 tablespoons) butter
4 fresh thyme sprigs
Kitchen string
5 cups (1½ pounds) peeled and thinly sliced parsnips

1 russet potato, peeled and chopped
½ cup thinly sliced celery
2 garlic cloves, minced
2½ teaspoons kosher salt
1½ teaspoons minced fresh ginger

3 cups reduced-sodium chicken broth
2 cups water
½ cup heavy cream
Garnishes: sour cream, fresh chives, olive oil

1. Remove and discard root ends and dark green tops of leeks. Cut in half lengthwise, and rinse thoroughly under cold running water to remove grit and sand. Cut into thin slices.

2. Melt the butter in a medium-size Dutch oven over medium. Tie the thyme sprigs together with kitchen string. Add the parsnips, next 5 ingredients, and thyme bundle to Dutch oven, and cook, stirring often, 10 minutes. Stir in the broth and 2 cups water, and bring to a boil. Reduce heat to medium-low; cover and simmer 15 minutes.

3. Discard the thyme bundle. Process the parsnip mixture, in batches, in a blender or food processor until smooth, stopping to scrape down sides as needed. Return the mixture to Dutch oven, and stir in heavy cream.

4. Cook over medium, stirring often, 5 minutes or until hot. Serve immediately.

NOTE: We tested with Swanson Natural Goodness 33% Less Sodium Chicken Broth.

CORNBREAD DRESSING

Freeze the unbaked dressing mixture in zip-top plastic freezer bags, making sure to press out excess air. Thaw in the refrigerator five days before Thanksgiving, and continue recipe with Step 6.

SERVES 10 to 12 per baking dish • **HANDS-ON:** 20 minutes
TOTAL: 3 hours, 20 minutes, including Cornbread Crumbles

BROTH:
- 14 cups reduced-sodium chicken broth
- 2 cups chopped celery
- 2 cups chopped sweet onion

CORNBREAD CRUMBLES:
- Vegetable cooking spray
- 3 cups self-rising white cornmeal mix
- 1 cup (4.5 ounces) all-purpose flour
- 2 tablespoons sugar
- 3 cups buttermilk
- 3 large eggs, lightly beaten
- 4 ounces (½ cup) butter, melted

- 1 (14-ounce) package herb-seasoned stuffing mix
- 2 cups cooked long-grain rice
- 8 large eggs, lightly beaten
- 2 tablespoons chopped fresh sage
- 2 tablespoons poultry seasoning
- 2 teaspoons freshly ground black pepper
- 1½ teaspoons table salt

1. Make the broth: Bring 8 cups of the chicken broth to a boil in a large Dutch oven over medium-high; stir in chopped celery and onion. Reduce heat to medium, and simmer 20 to 30 minutes or until celery and onion are very tender. Remove from heat, and stir in 4 cups of the chicken broth. Cool 30 minutes.

2. Make the crumbles: Preheat the oven to 425°F. Lightly grease a 13- x 9-inch baking pan with cooking spray. Stir together the cornmeal mix, flour, and sugar in a large bowl; whisk in buttermilk, eggs, and butter. Pour the batter into prepared pan.

3. Bake at 425°F for 30 minutes or until golden brown. Remove from oven, invert onto a wire rack, and cool completely (about 30 minutes). Crumble the cornbread.

4. Stir together the Cornbread Crumbles, stuffing mix, and rice in a very large bowl.

5. Reduce oven temperature to 350°F. Lightly grease 2 (13- x 9-inch) baking dishes with cooking spray. Stir the broth mixture, eggs, and next 4 ingredients into cornbread mixture until thoroughly combined. If needed, stir in up to 2 more cups of the chicken broth, ¼ cup at a time, until mixture is slightly soupy.

6. Spoon the mixture into prepared baking dishes. Bake at 350°F for 50 to 60 minutes or until done and top is light brown.

NOTE: We tested with Swanson Natural Goodness 33% Less Sodium Chicken Broth.

EASY BUTTER ROLLS

After Step 3, shape the dough into 1-inch balls, and place them on a baking sheet. Place baking sheet in freezer, and freeze completely. Transfer frozen balls to a large zip-top plastic freezer bag. The day before baking, remove from freezer, place three dough balls in each cup of a lightly greased muffin pan, cover with plastic wrap, and chill until ready to bake as directed.

MAKES 2 dozen · **HANDS-ON:** 30 minutes · **TOTAL:** 9 hours, 40 minutes

Vegetable cooking spray
1 cup milk
8 ounces (1 cup) butter
1 (¼-ounce) package active dry yeast

½ cup warm water (100° to 110°F)
½ cup plus 1 teaspoon sugar
2 large eggs

1 teaspoon table salt
5 cups bread flour

1. Lightly grease a large bowl with cooking spray. Heat the milk and ½ cup of the butter in a small saucepan over medium-low just until butter melts. Remove from heat, and cool mixture until a thermometer registers 100° to 110°F (about 10 minutes).
2. Stir together the yeast, ½ cup warm water (100° to 110°F), and 1 teaspoon of the sugar in a glass measuring cup, and let stand 5 minutes.
3. Beat the eggs at medium speed with a heavy-duty electric stand mixer; add remaining ½ cup sugar and 1 teaspoon salt, beating to combine. Add the milk mixture and yeast mixture, beating until combined. Reduce speed to low, and gradually add the flour, beating until blended. Place the dough in prepared bowl, turning to grease top. Cover with plastic wrap, and chill 8 hours to 5 days.
4. Lightly grease 2 (12-cup) muffin pans with cooking spray. Turn dough out onto a lightly floured surface, and knead 2 or 3 times. Gently shape dough into 72 (1-inch) balls.
5. Place 3 dough balls in each cup of prepared muffin pans. Microwave remaining ½ cup butter in a microwave-safe bowl at HIGH 1 minute or until melted. Brush rolls with half of the melted butter.
6. Cover muffin pans with plastic wrap, and let rise in a warm place (80° to 85°F), free from drafts, 45 minutes to 1 hour or until doubled in bulk.
7. Preheat the oven to 375°F. Bake the rolls at 375°F for 11 to 13 minutes or until golden brown. Brush with remaining melted butter.

SORGHUM BUTTER: Stir together 8 ounces (1 cup) softened butter and ½ cup sorghum syrup in a small bowl until blended. Serve immediately, or cover and chill up to 1 month. Makes 1½ cups

HERB BUTTER: Stir together 8 ounces (1 cup) softened butter, 2 teaspoons each chopped fresh thyme, sage, and parsley in a small bowl until blended. Serve immediately, or cover and chill up to 1 month. Makes 1 cup

PUMPKIN-ESPRESSO TIRAMISÙ

Loosely wrap baked and cooled tiramisù in plastic wrap, and refrigerate until ready to serve.

SERVES 10 to 12 • **HANDS-ON:** 45 minutes • **TOTAL:** 6 hours, 15 minutes

1   **cup granulated sugar**
1   **tablespoon all-purpose flour**
2   **large eggs**
2   **large egg yolks**
3   **cups heavy cream**
1   **teaspoon vanilla bean paste**

2   **(8-ounce) packages cream cheese, softened**
1   **cup canned pumpkin**
½   **cup brewed espresso or dark roast coffee**
3   **tablespoons brandy**

3   **(7-ounce) packages crisp ladyfingers, divided**
3   **tablespoons powdered sugar**
Garnish: ground nutmeg

1. Whisk together the sugar and flour in a large heavy saucepan. Whisk together the eggs, egg yolks, and 2 cups of the cream in a bowl. Whisk the cream mixture into sugar mixture, and cook over medium-low, whisking constantly, 15 minutes or until very thick. (Mixture will come to a simmer during the last 2 to 3 minutes.) Remove from heat; whisk in the vanilla bean paste, and transfer to a medium bowl. Place plastic wrap directly on warm custard (to prevent a film from forming). Cool completely (about 1½ hours).

2. Whisk the cream cheese into cream mixture until smooth; whisk in pumpkin.

3. Stir together the espresso and the brandy. Brush flat sides of about 24 ladyfingers with espresso mixture. Stand the ladyfingers around edge of a 10-inch springform pan, placing rounded sides against pan. Line bottom of pan with additional ladyfingers, cutting if necessary to cover bottom of pan completely. Brush the espresso mixture over ladyfingers on bottom of pan.

4. Spread one-third of the cream cheese mixture over ladyfingers on bottom. Repeat layers twice with remaining ladyfingers, espresso mixture, and cream cheese mixture, ending with cream cheese mixture. (Reserve any remaining ladyfingers for another use.) Cover and chill 4 hours to 2 days.

5. Beat remaining 1 cup cream at high speed with an electric mixer until foamy; gradually add powdered sugar, beating until soft peaks form. Dollop over cream cheese mixture.

NEW YEAR'S EVE SUPPER

Ring in a fresh start with a festive and satisfyingly simple soiree.

Menu

Southern 75

Spiked Satsuma Champagne

Gulf Coast Seafood Stew

Spiced Mayonnaise

Griddle Corn Cakes

Nutty Chocolate-Coconut Cake Bites

Tiny Caramel Tarts

SOUTHERN 75

MAKES 3½ cups · HANDS-ON: 5 minutes · TOTAL: 3 hours, 5 minutes

1 cup bourbon	⅓ cup powdered sugar	Garnishes: apple slices, lemon
½ cup lemon juice	2 cups chilled hard cider	twists, rosemary sprigs

Stir together bourbon, lemon juice, and powdered sugar in a pitcher until sugar dissolves (about 30 seconds). Cover and chill 3 hours to 24 hours. Divide among 8 Champagne flutes; top each with ¼ cup chilled hard cider.

NOTE: We tested with Angry Orchard hard cider.

SPIKED SATSUMA CHAMPAGNE

Frozen orange slices serve double duty as ice cubes and garnish in this bubbly elixir.

MAKES 9½ cups · HANDS-ON: 13 minutes · TOTAL: 43 minutes

2 satsumas, thinly sliced*	2 cups fresh satsuma orange	2 (750-milliliter) bottles
Wax paper	juice* (about 9 satsumas)	chilled dry Champagne
½ cup sugar	½ cup orange liqueur	

1. Arrange the orange slices on a baking sheet lined with wax paper; freeze 30 minutes.
2. Meanwhile, combine ½ cup water and the sugar in a 2-cup glass measuring cup. Microwave at HIGH 1 minute or until very hot. Stir until sugar dissolves.
3. Combine the sugar syrup, juice, and liqueur in a pitcher; chill until ready to serve.
4. Place 1 frozen orange slice in each Champagne glass. Pour ¼ cup juice mixture into each glass. Top with Champagne, and serve immediately.

* Fresh tangerines and bottled juice may be substituted. Look for both in the produce section.

GULF COAST SEAFOOD STEW

*This rustic stew was inspired by the rich, meaty flavors of a crawfish
or shrimp boil. Feel free to substitute more shrimp for the crawfish, if desired.*

SERVES 6 to 8 · HANDS-ON: 55 minutes
TOTAL: 1 hour, 35 minutes, not including corn cakes and mayonnaise

1½ pounds unpeeled, medium-size raw shrimp
2 celery ribs
1 large sweet onion
2 quarts reduced-sodium fat-free chicken broth
12 ounces andouille sausage, cut into ½-inch pieces
1 poblano pepper, seeded and chopped

1 green bell pepper, chopped
1 tablespoon canola oil
3 garlic cloves, chopped
1 pound small red potatoes, halved
1 (12-ounce) bottle beer
1 tablespoon fresh thyme leaves
2 fresh bay leaves
2 teaspoons Creole seasoning

1½ pounds fresh white fish fillets (such as snapper, grouper, or catfish), cubed
1 pound cooked crawfish tails (optional)
Kosher salt and pepper
Griddle Corn Cakes (recipe, page F91)
Spiced Mayonnaise (recipe, page F91)

1. Peel the shrimp; place the shells in a saucepan. (Refrigerate the shrimp until ready to use.) Add the celery ends and onion peel to pan; chop remaining celery and onion. (Using the leftover bits of onion and celery will layer the flavor and result in a flavorful broth.) Add the broth; bring to a boil over medium-high. Reduce the heat to low; simmer 30 minutes.

2. Meanwhile, cook the sausage in a large Dutch oven over medium-high, stirring often, 7 to 8 minutes or until browned. Remove the sausage; pat dry. Wipe the Dutch oven clean. Sauté the celery, onion, and peppers in hot oil in Dutch oven over medium-high 5 to 7 minutes or until onion is tender. Add the garlic, and sauté 45 seconds to 1 minute or until fragrant. Stir in the potatoes, next 4 ingredients, and sausage.

3. Pour the broth mixture through a fine wire-mesh strainer into Dutch oven, discarding the solids. Reserve ¼ cup broth for Spiced Mayonnaise recipe. Increase the heat to high; bring to a boil. Reduce the heat to low; cook, stirring occasionally, 20 minutes or until potatoes are tender.

4. Add the fish; cook 2 to 3 minutes or until just opaque. Add the shrimp, and cook 2 to 3 minutes or just until shrimp turn pink. If desired, stir in the crawfish, and cook 2 to 3 minutes or until hot. Discard the bay leaves. Add salt and pepper to taste.

5. Spoon the seafood into warmed soup bowls. Top with desired amount of the broth. Serve immediately with Griddle Corn Cakes and Spiced Mayonnaise.

SPICED MAYONNAISE

Portion control may be a problem, as this flavored mayo is so tasty that folks will want more. Feel free to double the recipe and use it just like plain mayonnaise.

MAKES 1 cup · HANDS-ON: 5 minutes · TOTAL: 10 minutes, not including broth

¼ cup Gulf Coast Seafood Stew broth (recipe, page F88)*
Pinch of ground saffron (optional)

1 cup mayonnaise with olive oil (such as Hellmann's with Olive Oil)

2 garlic cloves, minced

Stir together the broth and saffron, if desired; let stand 5 minutes. Stir together the mayonnaise and garlic in a small bowl. Whisk in broth mixture, 2 tablespoons at a time, until smooth and mixture is desired consistency.

* Bottled clam juice or chicken broth may be substituted.

GRIDDLE CORN CAKES

Smear the mayo over these cakes and encourage your guests to dunk them in the stew. Make them up to one hour ahead, and keep warm on low in the oven.

MAKES 20 · HANDS-ON: 10 minutes · TOTAL: 10 minutes

2 cups plain white or yellow cornmeal
1 teaspoon kosher salt

1 teaspoon baking soda
1 cup buttermilk
1 large egg, lightly beaten

¼ cup canola oil
1 scallion, thinly sliced

1. Stir together the first 3 ingredients in a small bowl.
2. Stir together the buttermilk, egg, and 2 tablespoons of the oil. Stir into the cornmeal mixture just until blended. Stir in the scallion.
3. Brush 1 tablespoon of the oil on a hot griddle. Drop cornmeal mixture by ⅛ cupfuls onto hot griddle. Flatten to ½ inch thick, and cook 1½ to 2 minutes on each side or until golden. Repeat process with the remaining batter and oil.

NUTTY CHOCOLATE-COCONUT CAKE BITES

Whether you call these truffles or cake bites, they're easy to make and fun to dip.

MAKES 8½ dozen · HANDS-ON: 58 minutes · TOTAL: 2 hours, 58 minutes

1 (18.25-ounce) package chocolate cake mix
1 (16-ounce) container milk chocolate ready-to-spread frosting

2 cups toasted coconut
1¾ cups toasted finely chopped pecans
Wax paper

4 (7-ounce) containers milk chocolate dipping chocolate
Candy dipping fork
Paper or aluminum foil baking cups

1. Prepare cake mix according to package directions in a lightly greased 13- x 9-inch pan. Let cool completely in the pan (about 30 minutes).

2. Crumble the cake into a bowl. Scoop frosting over crumbs. Sprinkle with 1 cup each of the coconut and pecans; stir gently just until thoroughly blended. Using a cookie scoop, scoop cake mixture into 1¼-inch balls; roll in hands, and place on wax paper-lined baking sheets. Cover and chill 1 hour.

3. Meanwhile, combine the remaining 1 cup coconut and ¾ cup pecans; stir well. Melt dipping chocolate, 1 container at a time, according to package directions; dip chilled balls in melted chocolate, using candy dipping fork and allowing excess chocolate to drip off. Place coated truffles on wax paper-lined baking sheets. Sprinkle with coconut-pecan mixture; chill 30 minutes or until set. Place truffles in baking cups.

TINY CARAMEL TARTS

Add a festive touch! Just before serving, sprinkle tarts with shaved chocolate, toffee, sea salt, or toasted pecans.

MAKES 6 dozen · HANDS-ON: 30 minutes · TOTAL: 4 hours, 30 minutes, including pastry shells

2 cups sugar
½ cup cold butter, sliced
6 tablespoons all-purpose flour
4 large egg yolks
2 cups milk

CREAM CHEESE PASTRY SHELLS:
1 cup butter, softened
1 (8-ounce) package cream cheese, softened

3½ cups all-purpose flour
Sweetened whipped cream

1. Cook 1 cup of the sugar in a medium-size heavy skillet over medium, stirring constantly, 6 to 8 minutes or until sugar melts and turns golden brown. Stir in the butter until melted.

2. Whisk together the flour, egg yolks, milk, and remaining 1 cup sugar in a 3-quart heavy saucepan; bring just to a simmer over low, whisking constantly. Add the sugar mixture to flour mixture, and cook, whisking constantly, 1 to 2 minutes or until thickened. Cover and chill 4 hours.

3. Meanwhile, prepare Cream Cheese Pastry Shells: Beat the butter and cream cheese at medium speed with a heavy-duty electric stand mixer until creamy. Gradually add the flour to butter mixture, beating at low speed just until blended. Shape the dough into 72 (¾-inch) balls, and place on a baking sheet; cover and chill 1 hour.

4. Preheat oven to 400°F. Place dough balls in lightly greased miniature muffin pans; press dough to top of cups, forming shells. Bake for 10 to 12 minutes. Remove from pans to wire racks, and cool completely (about 15 minutes). Spoon caramel mixture into shells, and top with whipped cream.